CHAOS TO CLARITY

Seeing the Signs and Breaking the Cycles

MARCI HOPKINS

The information in this book is a truthful recollection of actual events in the author's life.
The names and identifying characteristics of individuals and places may have been changed
to maintain anonymity.

An Imprint for GracePoint Publishing (www.GracePointPublishing.com)

GracePoint Matrix, LLC
624 S Cascade Ave
Suite 201
Colorado Springs, CO 80903
www.GracePointMatrix.com
Email: Admin@GracePointMatrix.com
SAN # 991-6032

A Library of Congress Control Number has been requested and is pending.

ISBN (Paperback): 978-1-955272-11-7
eISBN: 978-1-955272-12-4

Books may be purchased for educational, business, or sales promotional use.
For bulk order requests and price schedule contact:
Orders@GracePointPublishing.com

Disclaimer

The information provided in this book is strictly for informational purposes and is not intended as a substitute for advice from your physician or mental health provider. You should not use this information for diagnosis or treatment of any mental health problem.

Content Warning

This book contains writing that some readers may find disturbing, including incidents of child abuse, domestic violence, sexual abuse, and addiction.

Dedicated to my husband.

Thank you for showing me what true love is and
supporting me through my healing journey.

TABLE OF CONTENTS

PREFACE

I felt called to write this book for those still struggling in a battle against addiction, anxiety, depression, self-hatred, substance abuse, sexual trauma, and more. It is a book about owning behaviors and habits from the past and moving from victim to survivor. It's about uncovering the root beneath addiction. More importantly, it is a guide to offer a new possibility for your future, health, and well-being. I will not pretend to be someone I am not by acting like I have all the answers, yet I am eager to share my story and my journey to healing. I am excited to offer you options to take your first steps whether you are thinking of recovery, in a program already, or just wanting to create a better future for yourself. This book is about discovering and finding yourself again.

Chaos to Clarity is about seeing and recognizing the signs in your life that signal discomfort, disappointment, and unhappiness. I have broken generational cycles of abuse and trauma and I offer you ways to do the same. It is about breaking the chains of our lineage and redirecting future generations toward peace and prosperity through our choices and actions. It is my commitment to pave a new way of life and shine a light of hope to those who have been trapped in the darkness of pain, addiction, self-sabotage, and more, for far too long. I want to share that I am living proof that recovery and breaking negative cycles are possible.

This book is also filled with guidance, invitations, and opportunities to reflect throughout, and at the end, there are exercises and resources. I have chosen to write this book not to position myself as some expert or guru, but rather to meet you where you are and let you know that I have been there too. You are *not* alone, even when you feel more isolated than ever. There are people like me who champion others as they start the path to being better people. There is community and support available. I would love to walk with you, even for a moment, along your journey to sobriety, happiness, peace, contentment, and joy for life again.

I hope to offer you a new lease on life by providing an opportunity to take on the work shared in these pages. I am giving you everything I've learned, with the desire to give you everything you've hoped for.

It is a guide for healing from your past, making amends in relationships, walking in faith, and creating your most fulfilling life. This was a truly cathartic experience and has helped me to further my healing, move past my trauma, discover my purpose in this life, and live in joy.

There is so much goodness that awaits you through the healing journey. Welcome to your very first step.

PART 1

Chaos

1

Where the Chaos Began

They must have had another party night, I think to myself, waiting around in Tim's roommate's room. *They always sleep in really late. I don't like sleeping here. There's nothing to do here and I don't like sleeping alone. I want to play. I want my mommy.*

The sun is up. When's Mommy waking up? How much longer? I wonder as I sit up and look for something to play with. *I don't want to lie in bed anymore. I want to go outside. I really want my mommy. Why does she have to take so long?*

As I look around the room, it's just a bunch of grown-up stuff: clothes, a desk, posters on the walls. No toys, no kid stuff, no fun… *Ah! Candy!*

Tootsie Rolls. I love Tootsie Rolls, so I run over to grab the can in the closet and it's heavy. I pop the top off and I realize it's not candy. *It's full of money!* I gasp at the sight, look up at the door, and pour all of them out on the floor. I don't know what coins they are exactly, but I do know that the silver ones are worth more than the brown ones, so I begin to separate them.

I wonder how much this is, I think as I stack the silver coins together and put the brown ones back into the Tootsie Roll can. *The can didn't have Tootsie Rolls, but maybe I can buy some now. Maybe Tim will think his roommate took the coins and I won't be blamed.* I am a little nervous about it, but I think to myself, *what if no one knows and I get to keep them? That would be great!*

Where the heck is Mommy? Come on already! Time just keeps passing by and I keep sitting around in this boring room. I'm so bored. The morning feels like it's taking forever, and I want to know when Mommy is going to wake up. I just want to play with her. I miss her.

Tim bursts through the door, "Marci, I have something for you."

He scares me. I don't like my mom's boyfriend. Being around him makes my stomach hurt and I don't like being stuck at his house, especially when I don't get to play with Mommy. "What is it?" I ask timidly.

"It's a bank," he replies with a smile.

Oh no, I think. *He's grabbing the Tootsie Roll can.* My heart stops. *Oh, no.*

His smile fades quickly the moment he picks it up. He shakes it, confused because it's so light, and opens it. His smile is completely gone now.

"Where's the money?" he asks, now frowning.

"I... I don't know." I say back, no longer able to look straight at him.

Oh no, I think to myself. I take a big gulp, but my throat feels tight. I want to cry but I don't want him to know it was me. I don't want to get in trouble. I keep wondering where my mom is and hoping she'll walk in. Tim is scaring me. He looks so angry and big.

"Marci, there were a lot of coins in here and now they are gone. What did you do with them?" His voice gets louder with each word, and I know he is mad at me. I don't know what he is going to do but I want to run and hide.

"I don't know! I didn't take anything! What coins?" I was trembling inside. I knew what coins, but I couldn't put them back at that moment. *I wish I hadn't done that, and I am so scared of Tim's yelling. I just want to get away.*

"Marci! Let's go tell your mother," he says angrily as he grabs my arm and pulls me out of the room. I cry as he squeezes my arm, dragging me down the hallway and marching me into his room where

Mommy is lying on the bed. There she is. After all this time, she's just lying here. I want to run to her. I want her to run to me. I am crying out loud, but I am screaming to her in my head, *Mommy, please save me. PLEASE!* but she doesn't move. She just stays there.

"Tell your mother what you did!" he shouts, hovering over me with his fists clenched.

I can hardly get a word out between my tears, "Nothing!"

"What happened?" Mommy asks us both. I want her to get up and grab me. I want to go. I want her to save me from her stupid boyfriend. *Why do we have to live here?* I want us to leave here.

"Your daughter stole the money from the bank I was going to give her!" He is shouting at both of us. He is still leaning over me, so angry. His face is red and as soon as he tells on me, my heart sinks. I feel so ashamed and embarrassed. I don't want Mommy to be mad at me either.

"Marci? Is this true?" she asks in her soft voice.

"Yes, I'm sorry. I was bored. I didn't know…" I couldn't finish my sentence because Tim hits me so hard, I can't speak. I forget where I am because I see a flash. I don't know what is happening, but he keeps hitting me, over and over. It's too much: the yelling, the hitting, the crying. I can't catch my breath. Between tears, I am begging for it to stop. I am screaming for Mommy to make it stop and she is just lying there, watching. I can't understand why she won't make it stop.

"Marci, come with me," she finally gets up and starts walking out of the room. Tim drops me from his grip, and I fall. My whole body hurts, and I can't think or see straight. I can hardly see through my tears. I can't catch my breath or stop crying and screaming. My butt hurts so bad; it hurts to walk.

"Marci, calm down. It will be okay," she says to me as she holds me. I am finally with her, just sobbing in her arms. She is trying to make me stop crying but I can't. I am so sad. I am confused and broken. It hurts so bad.

"MOMMY, I'M SORRY. MOMMY!" I cannot stop crying. I am in so much pain. My heart hurts as much as my butt. *Why didn't*

Mommy stop Tim? Why?

"You can't do things like that Marci. It's wrong."

"I know, Mommy." I cannot stop crying. My whole body hurts now. My head, my eyes, my throat. I am choking on my tears. I'm so scared of what just happened.

"Sweetie, please stop crying. You know we are going to your grandparents today."

"Yes, Mommy."

"You can't tell your grandparents about this. They would be very upset."

"Okay, Mommy" the tears will not stop. *She wants me to keep this a secret? Why didn't she help me?* It hurts too much to pretend. I don't understand why this had to happen.

"Please don't do anything like this again, honey."

"Okay, Mommy. I am sorry."

"It had to be done," Tim tells her meanly. "She had to learn a lesson."

"Okay," I hear Mommy say back to him. I hate him.

I'll never forget that day for as long as I live. My first spanking changed me forever. I still have flashbacks of this memory whenever I see a Tootsie Roll. I get a shiver up my spine when I think about the pain that little six-year-old me endured. A young child, left unattended all morning to fend for herself, keeping herself entertained while her hungover mother slept in and did drugs. There is still so much pain in this memory that it was difficult to retell for the purposes of this book, and yet, here we are.

A part of my childlikeness disappeared that day. I lost something, never to be returned. When I think about it, it was the hope, the spark, the naive innocence that was whipped right out of me and it felt like my spirit left my body. I was hollow inside. I felt far away from everything in my reality; mostly, I felt a certain abandonment by my mom.

It is burned into my memory the way she just sat there, still and seemingly unfazed. I felt so alone, even with her just inches away from me. I couldn't believe that she let it happen and that she let someone hurt me. In hindsight, I think she must have been just as scared as I was. I think she was afraid to intervene and get hit too.

After that day, my hope and trust in her were inaccessible. I don't exactly know where it went, but I never found it again. Little did I know she would do this for years to come. She would let men abuse and traumatize me for years without ever stepping in.

I didn't even have time to process what had just happened because we had plans to go to my grandparents' house for a party later that day. I was in physical and emotional pain, and my backside was already showing black and blue marks. At first, I tried to keep it to myself, but I was so upset with both of them that I took the first opportunity I had to show my grandma. I remember being in the laundry room with her for a moment and I showed her my behind. I was crying, she was crying, but she was also very angry. I was glad she was as upset as I was.

When my grandma told my grandfather, he was furious as well. They were both so distressed that they made my mom and Tim leave immediately. I was still in physical pain, but I was relieved to feel an ounce of justice being served. My mom didn't stick up for me or stop the beating but at least my grandparents came to my rescue.

Later in life, my aunt told me that when they left, I stuck my tongue out at my mom. I have no doubt. I'm sure I felt like I got my revenge. I mean, what else would I do at six years old? I am sure I wanted to do much worse but felt so powerless in the situation. I was grateful to have the protection of my grandma, grandpa, and aunts. I didn't always have their protection as I grew into an adult and started making my own decisions, but at age six, loving family was everything I needed.

2

To Grandmother's House We Go

I stayed with my grandparents that night and they told me I could stay longer if I wanted to. They didn't want me living around Tim and their partying lifestyle so at six years old, they asked me to make the decision to live with them or my mom. This sort of took me by surprise.

Can you imagine a six-year-old being given the choice of where to live? How could I decide something like that? Being faced with this decision made me sick to my stomach. I was being asked to choose between my mother and grandparents. There I was, a young girl, having to weigh the pros and cons of both choices. Feeling safe and loved was a top priority and that was what drove me to choose my grandparents, but it broke my heart to come to that conclusion. I hated the feeling of questioning the love of my mother. All I wanted was to be loved and give love, which is what we all want and need in our most formative years. But to thrive, we must also have safety, shelter, and bit of predictability. I would have given anything to live with my mom in a safe home and have her love, but it wasn't that simple. That wasn't one of my options.

After a few days, when it came time to make my decision to live with my grandparents, I vividly recall standing in my grandma's room on the phone next to her bed. I was looking out over the family room, telling my mom I wasn't coming back to Tim's and that I was staying with grandma. I cried the whole time through that phone call.

I see the scene in my mind's eye, but I don't remember what was said over the phone. The stress of that conversation sort of blurred the words that were exchanged. I can't fully recall her response when I told her I was staying at Grandma's for good, I just remember that she didn't exactly beg me to come home. I hung up the phone feeling lost and numb. Realizing she didn't save me, didn't leave Tim for me, left me literally sick to my stomach.

It felt like a lot of pressure at that age to decide with whom to live. It was a huge weight on my chest, and it made me so scared. Of course, I wanted to live with my mom, but not her boyfriend, and choosing my grandparents made me feel guilty. I spent many nights crying about this guilt and pain, wishing, praying, and begging for things to be different.

In my youth, I hated being shuffled around. My mom was still in my life and the back and forth between houses every week made me feel nauseous. It was hard to find a sense of home or real joy because all I ever wanted was to feel like my mom chose me over her boyfriend and her addiction, which never happened. She always chose the party lifestyle. She stayed at Tim's, and I lived with my grandparents.

I walked out of my grandparents' room after that call and right into the embrace of my grandmother, and my new life began. I was so scared of what I'd done, but at least I felt safe, sobbing in her arms. I am forever grateful that my grandparents took me in, but I always wondered what it would be like if things were different, if I had a more typical or functional upbringing.

I also wondered what this new life was going to be like. *Would my mom be around at all? Would she still claim me? Would I ever go back over to Tim's? Would she ever leave Tim?* I had so many questions and some of them were answered over time. I ended up living with my grandparents until twelve.

My grandparents gave me a great life. My grandma enrolled me in school and made sure I had everything I needed to succeed. She had a heart of gold. I was so grateful they offered to raise me. They gave me the most normal life they could during that time. School, after-school activities, family dinners, and vacations included. I would have never had that lifestyle and stability with my mom. She was an immature nineteen-year-old when she had me, still figuring life out, and should have probably been living at home and still being raised by her parents herself, but that wasn't her way.

My mom was the oldest of four children, and her sisters still lived at home with their parents, my grandparents. I felt like I had siblings taking care of me. Growing up, I was often reminded by them that they *raised* me, but I often felt like I grew up *with* them.

I grew up in what I now know were dysfunctional settings, but I would say that I always adapted and learned how to make it work. I developed survival tactics at a very young age to make it through the chaos of my life. I subconsciously learned to avoid mental, emotional, and physical pain by swapping out my life for another one. It started subconsciously when choosing to live with my grandparents and it developed into a skill as I aged. I moved schools every two years. I moved houses as a child and teen over seven times and this created a pattern of changing my life when life wasn't going the way I wanted. This strategy stayed with me to avoid pain. I couldn't always describe it this way, especially the ages and phases when I was just trying to find my way, but now, I can see it clearly. Now, I watch out for that urge to run and start over.

I have many stories of traumatic experiences that no child should endure. Alcohol was around all the time, included in every situation, but it didn't stand out as strange to me. It was just a part of life, normal. There were other adult things happening around me, and sometimes, I found myself a part of them. This included drinking mixed with explicit grown-up conversations and behavior. Living with my grandparents seemed like my best option, though far from perfect; it was the best I could get.

I remember the familiar sting of disappointment many times over the course of my life. I often longed for my mother, but she was usually off doing her own thing. From a very young age, I understood that my mom liked partying and men, and I always felt she chose them over me. My mother faced, or rather avoided, her own demons with alcohol, drugs, and men and had very low self-esteem, which directly affected me and our connection. Her relationships with men were more important than anything because, to her, they validated her worth. I know that now. As a daughter, who needed her mother's validation, this was very hard to navigate.

My mom had me at nineteen and my dad was twenty-three. My parents were only married for a year, and my dad was hardly in my life after he left us. He, too, was a hippie, but a perpetual one. His entire life revolved around motorcycles, weed, and alcohol. He even lived above a bike mechanic shop.

From what I have been told, my mom was very shy, sheltered, and withdrawn until she met my dad. They went to prom together and were high school sweethearts. My mom grew up very quickly dating a man four years older than her and started acting a lot older when he exposed her to more. She discovered drugs at her first Janis Joplin concert with him. There was no turning back for her.

When she got pregnant with me at eighteen, they tried to do the right thing and married, but it didn't work for them. Addiction and financial issues became too much of a challenge for their relationship to overcome. Eventually, this left me with my mom, who was still interested in partying. My father's absence had a huge impact on my life and relationship with men. It has cost me much over the years. While my grandparents provided for my basic needs and my aunts became my sisters, great damage was already done.

The nervous system develops through childhood. If children don't experience safe, predictable, and secure relationships (usually with their primary caregivers), the body learns that people are not safe. This leads to many behavioral issues including a variety of addictions, maladaptive coping mechanisms, codependent relationships, disconnection between brain and body, self-esteem issues, and much more. People grow up seeking an idea of what they believe will make them safe yet repeating many of the patterns encoded in the biology of the nervous system from childhood. When we survive something, it becomes familiar, and the brain will categorize it as "safe" because we lived through it. Oddly, those dysfunctional relationships, activities, and choices are often what we seek out despite our "knowing" that they are no good for us. I know that now, but did not then.

3

Fairy Tale Family

My mother spent her whole adult life trying to replace my father and because of it, I was forced to deal with a lot of crappy men. I never liked her boyfriends, and especially didn't enjoy moving in with them. There was always partying and fighting. I thought this would go on forever, but things started looking up when my mom *finally* left Tim.

I couldn't have been happier. I was so glad for her to get away from him. I was sure our troubles were over when she eventually met the man who I thought was our knight in shining armor, Richard Dick. *Yes. Richard. Dick.*

He seemed like the kindest, most loving man I'd ever met. He was so good to my mom and me. He was our very own Prince Charming and this idea filled me with hope. He was a tall, handsome man, and I was happy for my mom. I was happy for me. He was a fun guy. We went to dinners and shopped together, we played games and traveled. He had a successful business and was able to provide a great lifestyle for us. This finally made me feel safe and even more excited for the future.

I thought I was going to finally have the perfect life every kid dreams of: a fairy tale family. I was going to have a dad like I had prayed for. I thought I would get my mom back and we were going to become a stable family. I felt like we were going to be living happily ever after, just doing what real families did. I was so thrilled for the promise of their relationship and how much better it was going to make our lives.

Things moved quickly between my mom and Richard. When they got engaged, I was overjoyed! To me, it was officially the rest of *our* happy lives. I was their number one cheerleader. I loved seeing my mom happy and I felt safe with two parents. I felt *normal*; I believed all the other kids in school lived this way, and I was elated to finally have this for myself.

Their wedding was at my grandparents' house. It was a small event but to me, it was the best day of my life. Everyone was happy, having lots of fun, and drinking quite a bit—including me.

I was offered champagne and I remember really liking the way it made me feel. Soon enough, I drank too much, and someone—I'm not sure who—had to put me to bed. When I woke up the next day, nothing happened. I didn't get a lecture about the negative effects of alcohol. I didn't get in trouble, and no one even told me it was bad or wrong. No one said anything about a twelve-year-old getting champagne wasted at her mom's wedding. No one made it a big deal. Drinking was just acceptable in my family.

This is when drinking started for me. It became normal and acceptable on a new level. Based on what I observed, drinking was as ordinary as eating, and in my adult years, sometimes I drank more than I ate. After their wedding, I knew I wasn't going to have to answer to anyone about drinking so I started to explore and use it more in the coming years.

It was also in the early years of my mom's marriage to Richard that would give me reason to drink. In the beginning of their relationship, I thought I had hit the jackpot. We were living in a beautiful condominium in Spring Branch, Texas. We had money, lived in a nice area, and I had my mom and a new dad. I loved it.

I also moved to a new school in the middle of seventh grade. I made my way through school making friends. I'd gotten good at making new friends because I was always moving—every two years to be exact. Moving homes and schools was something I had grown used to. I never got too close to anyone because if it didn't work out, I knew I could move on. Only in retrospect, I understand now how this shaped my inability to form true bonds with others. I was always ready for a new life, a do-over. I have countless stories of attempts to start over any time my drinking got too severe, or life got too hard (more on that later).

I thought we finally had it all figured out after years of suffering. I liked my new life and new school. My stepdad was nice, but then things got uncomfortable, quickly. With Tim, I didn't feel safe because of the beatings. The difference was his physical abuse was overt and aggressive. Richard's abuse was covert and confusing.

I felt like Richard was becoming a real dad to me until one day in seventh grade, he took me to see *Porky's*. That seems unusual to me now as an adult but at the time, I thought he was cool for letting me go see an R-rated movie.

We were sitting in the theater and there were very few people because it was the middle of the afternoon. As we were watching the movie, he had his arm around me. Initially, I felt safe. I remember thinking how lucky I was. I always wanted a dad who claimed me, a father figure who loved me, accepted me, and held me but this wasn't the same kind of holding I was daydreaming about; it was icky.

He was a large man at six feet tall and over 200 pounds. That was particularly large compared to my five-foot, four-inch, hundred-pound frame. His big arm wrapped all the way around me and not too far into the movie, he put his hand on my knee. This caught my attention. It didn't feel right. Inner alarms sounded, dully at first. Then, he started moving his hand up my leg. This disconcerted me immediately.

I started having a rush of panicked thoughts. *What is he doing? What is he thinking? What is happening right now?* I started to lose my breath and froze for a second. He was slowly moving his hand further up my thigh; he was trying to touch me between my legs.

After a moment of complete shock and doing nothing, sitting

frozen in what I now know is the "freeze" reaction of the sympathetic nervous system, I freaked out and started to resist; I started to fight. I tried to push his hand away from me, but he continued his attempt. After what felt like forever, I finally got out of his grip and ran out of the theater crying as I fled from the enemy. I was outside, hysterical, when he found me. He was trying to calm me and bring me down from my panic, but I was extremely upset. I was surprised and embarrassed and grossed out. I wouldn't listen to him or calm down. I was disturbed by his actions. I was nauseated. I could not contain my complete and utter disgust.

He probably thought I was just reacting to the situation but there was yet another layer of pain to this experience. He had just crushed my hopes of ever having my fairy tale family. At that moment, my whole dream of our new life came crashing down. He was no prince. He was a pervert. I was devastated.

I could hardly even look at him, but he started apologizing profusely and I wouldn't have it. "Marci, Marci, calm down, please," he pleaded. I wailed harder. I cried out tears of hate, disgust, and disappointment and that is when the offering of gifts started. "Marci... Marci, you wanted to go on that trip to Europe, yes?" he asked, still pleading, but I hiccupped when that caught my attention. "Yeah, yeah," he said, realizing he had struck something in me.

"Well, how about we go get you some luggage for that trip, huh? Yeah..." I started to calm down and he continued to apologize for the offense. I was rattled by all that had just happened, confused at his actions then his offer of gifts, but I let him take me to get the luggage. I was in a whirlwind of thoughts, fears, concerns, and emotions, so I just agreed to his suggestion. He took me to buy luggage and promised it would never happen again. I wanted to believe him.

That day, I went home with new luggage and a new secret, but I was also distracted by my excitement to go on that trip. He knew I wanted to go on that trip for months and suddenly, I was allowed to go. We didn't talk about it anymore, and I shifted my attention to Europe. It was six months away, but it was also a chance to get away from him and out of that house. The trip couldn't come fast enough.

To survive the kind of trauma I had experienced in my life, I became extremely skilled at putting things out of my mind. Events were placed in a box and tucked neatly away, never to be opened. I had to forget that things happened to me. From that first beating from Tim, to watching my mom verbally and physically fight with all her boyfriends, I had to keep showing up to each new day like nothing happened. There was no way I could hold onto so much of it or I think it would have just completely broken me down to nothing—which eventually happened much later in my adult years. As a young girl, the only way to survive was to try to forget.

There are many events and stories that I will share in this book that came back to full memory *because* of writing this book—because I became clear. As a means of survival from a mental breakdown or tipping into insanity, the brain will automatically compartmentalize or black out certain memories to protect us. I healed a lot of pain in my sobriety journey. It was also in writing this book that I was able to sort out so many of the things I had previously forgotten. So much became clear from my years of chaos.

Something that I was trying to both ignore and forget was the way that Richard made advances at me while my mom wasn't around. He didn't try to touch me again like at the movies, but he showed me pictures of women or talked about the porn he watched and would tell me, "If you looked like that, I would leave your mother."

I was doing everything I could to survive this part of my life, but I hated it. I figured I couldn't tell my mom because she had always left me on my own. She never came to my rescue so my trip to Europe was my mental escape. I dreamed of it; I counted down the days for it. I was just trying to enjoy school and get away from home as much as possible to minimize any chance I had at being alone with him.

Another reason I kept wanting to escape was because I was becoming pretty sure that Richard was coming into my room at night. I never had any proof, but I had this feeling about it. He was coming onto me strongly and persistently, but I couldn't prove it. It was in the way he looked at me, the way his gaze lingered, and the way he spoke. He didn't stop making passes, but he had become more subtle in his approach. I had no proof of what I thought was happening, so I didn't say anything. I sometimes wondered if I was crazy. I was just trying to make it through the months until Europe.

Flash forward: My time in Europe was the trip of a lifetime with friends from school, and I was grateful that I got to go on it. It was a break from the chaos at home and as soon as I got back, my mom and Richard informed me that we would be going on another trip to Singapore and Hong Kong, just the three of us. I was thrilled about this news! There I was, a girl who had never been out of Houston, suddenly on two international trips in one summer. I was on top of the world!

We went on the second trip just a week after I got back from Europe. Singapore was amazing. We had great fun as a family on that leg of the trip. I had done my best to put the thought of Richard touching me out of my mind, and I felt like we were getting back to being a family again. I even wondered if it was true, or if I had exaggerated everything I'd felt before. I was endlessly committed to the hope of that fairy tale family. I wanted to let my dream of happily ever after return. I wanted to feel whole. I wanted to love and be loved, and it seemed like that could possibly happen.

We left Singapore and headed to Hong Kong. It was another amazing place, and we spent the first day by the pool at the hotel. We were going to dinner that night at a nice restaurant that I was excited about. I was reaching my teen years and my looks were very important to me. Knowing it took me a while to get ready, I wanted to go back to the room a bit early to shower, get dressed, do my make-up, and straighten my hair.

Richard walked me back to the room because he wanted to lie down, and my mom stayed at the pool. While I went to take a shower, he rested. The hotel bathroom had a large shower shaped in a square glass cube. The fixtures were fancy, and the bathroom door had wooden slats that tilted up.

At one point, I looked at the door and I saw Richard squatting down, looking up the slats. He was watching me shower! I lost my breath at the sight of him peeking at me and experienced that same panic I felt in the movie theater. I felt frozen and hysterical all over again.

Immediately, I jumped out of the shower soaking wet. I started to cry and freak out, trying to cover my body. I squatted down into the fetal position to hide and make the feeling go away. I felt overwhelmed by a rush of fear. I was screaming internally. *Why? Why is this happening to me?* I just wanted it to stop so badly. I stayed there for a few minutes, and it felt like an eternity.

I began to catch my breath again and made sure he was gone. I remember seeing his shadow leave and I slowly got back in the shower to rinse off, but I was terrified. I didn't want him to come back. I felt gross. Exposed. Vulnerable. I tried to hurry and finish, constantly watching for him through the door slats.

When I finished, I felt sick to my stomach and scared to death about what to do. I got out and dried off, checking the slats to make sure he hadn't come back. Scared and nauseated, I started putting my makeup on, hidden in the bathroom afraid to face Richard. I just kept wondering what I was going to do. What was I supposed to do? I figured I'd act like nothing happened. I didn't know who I could tell. To protect myself and my mom, I guessed that keeping it to myself and pretending it didn't happen was all I could do.

I was crying quietly to myself, and when my mom finally got back, she came into the bathroom abruptly. I was half dressed. She told me Richard wanted to be alone and she insisted we leave immediately. I told her I wasn't done getting ready and refused to leave. She fought back and insisted I get out of the bathroom. I argued with her and made it about wanting to get ready but, in truth, I was terribly angry and upset by the whole shower situation. My frustration grew because I had to leave with wet hair.

Not paying much attention to the state I was in, my mom said it was fine that I didn't get to do my hair and that we would try to find a place to blow it out somewhere in the hotel. I was furious but we left. We were walking around the hotel aimlessly, all because Richard wanted alone time. He had tried to look at me nude and had kicked *us* out of our own room. God only knew what he was doing while my mom and I walked around fighting. I was seething.

She was trying hard to find a place for me to finish getting ready but there was nothing. We had walked around outside with no plan. My anger was growing and so was my attitude with her. I kept talking back, and she snapped at me every moment. The tension between us kept heating up.

She dragged me along as I resisted her, and we arrived at these walkways over the water in the courtyard. We had walked down one, screaming at each other. At the peak of our argument, she turned around and started choking me. I couldn't believe what she was doing. Her hands around my neck flipped a switch in me and I no longer had a reason to hold back.

I screamed at the top of my lungs, "I can't believe you are protecting a man that is sexually abusing me!" She released her grip and took a step back as if I had pushed her away with my words. I could see the shock on her face. There was silence.

"What are you talking about?" She muttered, visibly in dismay by what she had just heard.

I told her about the movie theater and what had happened. I told her that I thought he was coming into my room at night and touching me in my sleep. I told her about what happened upstairs just minutes before. I was crying and yelling at the same time. I was so mad at her and yet, wanted her to save me from what I was experiencing. The pain from the whole situation was tearing me apart and I was still so raw from the shower incident. I was so afraid to tell her and couldn't keep my secret for another second.

What happened next broke my spirit in a way I can hardly put into words.

"Marci, I cannot afford to leave him. You are just going to have to wear more clothes to bed."

There is not much more I remember.

I think I blacked out if anything else was said. My mother was not going to save me. Again. She was not going to save *us*. I lost all hope in that moment and a part of me went dark. I was crushed.

We went back to the room and like so many times in our lives, we acted like nothing happened. The Marci that returned to that room was not the Marci that left it. A shell of a girl went back, numb to the pain and heartbreak she was experiencing.

I still don't understand how she stayed. I can't fathom how she could look at him knowing what he was doing to her daughter. I knew she struggled with her worth. I could tell that her inner demons ran deep, but I arrived at a new low with her when not even her daughter's sexual abuse would end a toxic relationship.

From that night on, I went to bed wearing more clothes. I felt vulnerable and scared. It was unfair to have to be in such dangerous living conditions. To me, sleep should be the safest time. Instead, I was forcing myself to stay up later than him and I usually fell asleep without knowing it. I did my best to stay up as late as I could, but I was *so* tired often. I was trying to be my own watch guard but failing to stay awake.

My fairy tale family dreams were a living nightmare.

It wasn't until I was healing in my adult years that I learned the term *grooming*. This is a term used to describe the behavior of a sexual predator to condition the person they are pursuing: their prey. An abuser will slowly and subtly gain the trust of their target and coerce them into sexual acts that would normally be alarming to the target.

However, because the act of grooming is slow and calculated, the abuser gains a closeness and trust with their victim to justify or normalize the sexual abuse to reduce the risk of getting caught. The abuser will encourage secrets and give incentives, such as gifts, to withhold what is going on.

At that age, I truly didn't understand what I was in the middle of. I can only see the grooming in retrospect, as an adult. In theory, that is the point: the subtlety of it. I only know this is what happened to me because I learned the term and did my research. I realized through my research why I was targeted by my stepfather.

He saw that I was vulnerable, had emotional neediness, came from chaos, and had very little parental oversight. As a result, he began giving me special attention. He filled so many needs that I had been seeking and as a family, we all had complete trust in him.

From this vantage point, it seems clear that there were many premeditated situations in my time with him, like going to see an adult movie alone together. I feel sickened by the idea that this was a plan. From *his* vantage point, Richard found many times we could be alone. He knew that I was seeking his love and attention and he used that to his advantage.

Again, from the context of grooming, he took me swimming many times, which gave him the chance to see me as close to naked as he could get away with. Whenever he had the opportunity, he showed me pictures and discussed porn with me to sexualize our relationship. He was sort of training, conditioning, and desensitizing me about sexuality.

The clearest signal that all of this was grooming was that we had our secret. I felt there would be huge consequences if I said something. I finally had a beautiful life and so did my mom. I thought I could keep my secret, it would go away, and I wouldn't have to destroy what my mom and I now had.

The worst, and most detrimental part, is how damaging grooming is for a child. I wanted to die because I saw no way out. I was failing all my classes. Because I was failing, I was grounded by Richard for six weeks at a time in a home where I did not feel safe. It was an emotional prison.

When I wasn't grounded, the only refuge I had was playing video games at the corner store. I kept everything perfect on the outside—my hair, clothes, and makeup—while the inside was dying. I did this as a child to protect the secret, but I was groomed to think I had no other options and no way out.

4

The Shift

As an adult, I wrote a poem called "The Shift." It is about the shift that occurred during my years of enduring sexual trauma. It is about the transition that happened after realizing my mother wasn't going to fight for me, save me, or get us out of the situation we were in.

Before sharing the poem, I would like to explain more about the impact of sexual abuse on a person's development. There can be healing, therapy, counseling, and more but the damage done by abuse is irreversible. We can heal, but the scar remains.

It is natural that when we are young, we look to the adults in our life for support, love, and guidance. When someone we love begins to touch us in a way we don't understand or approve of, we may first wonder why, but we don't know what to do. It is not in alignment with how we feel about that person as a trusted individual. When a trusted adult abuses that trust, it can cause issues that plague our relationships indefinitely.

It can be shocking, as our mind is trying to process what is happening. *How could this happen? Why would this happen? How could this person do this to me? What did I do to deserve this?* The predator's actions do not fit how that child needs them as a trusted adult figure, and this can have such a lasting, negative impact on a young person trying to make sense of it all.

When we are put in a position of sexuality at a young age, there is a shift. When someone who is supposed to be a protector begins to touch a child, that child's perspective of what is appropriate love from a man, woman, or grown-up gets skewed. The entire understanding and perspective of love changes.

A child's perspective of themselves changes. There is a shift in the whole value system. This is when many subjects of abuse conclude that their value lies in their looks, performance, or other similar features. It is natural to then equate love to the attention received for what is provided rather than who the person is.

We may think and hope that things can go back to the way they were, but they can't. The abuse may come to an end, but it has a long-term effect. An individual may shift from feeling like a victim to a survivor of abuse but that does not remove the memory or the shifts it caused. It also does not reverse any damage already done.

Oftentimes, victims of abuse are forced to mature much sooner than those who have not faced such treatment. These were signs that I wish the adults in my life would have noticed and acted on. If you are also a survivor of sexual abuse, you may recognize some of these shifts and changes within yourself. You may also find this information to be new to you. It may teach you things you didn't know about yourself and the way that abuse affected you. This is an opportunity for yet another layer of processing and healing, both for you and for the next generation.

Some signs typical for younger children who have lived through abuse may include displaying regressive behaviors such as bed-wetting or thumb sucking, suddenly having new words for private body parts, or resisting removing clothing at appropriate times such as bath time, bedtime, toileting, or diapering. Some other examples young children may present could include asking other children to behave sexually or play sexual games, or mimicking adult sexual behaviors with toys, stuffed animals, or drawing/storytelling.

Some signs to watch out for with children include newly

occurring nightmares or other sleep problems without an explanation or seeming distracted or distant (dissociation). It is important to know a child's eating habits because they can also reveal a subtle shift. There could be something wrong if they have a sudden change in eating habits, refusal to eat, or have a drastic loss or increase in appetite.

With older children, it may be hard to detect sexual abuse as the cause, but a symptom can be sudden mood swings of rage, fear, insecurity, or withdrawal. They may attempt to communicate as best they can by doing things that seem likely to provoke a discussion about sexual issues. They may write, draw, or enact sexual or frightening imagery. They are doing their best to communicate with us, and we must observe and listen.

A sign to watch for is when children develop new or unusual fears or distrust of certain people or places. This one can be the most telling. Some other tells include refusal to talk about a secret shared with an adult or older child, talking about a new older friend, or suddenly having money, toys, or other gifts without reason.

Another hint that something could be happening is when a child or teen suddenly has no interest in hygiene and appearances, especially if previously, they did care. This can be an external portrayal of an internal belief that the child caused the abuse, so they want to be dirty and unattractive to avoid this sort of behavior in the future. This can also be a reason for excessive weight gain in children/teens (an unconscious way of repelling an adult: if I look ugly, am overweight and dirty, no one will want my body). The reverse is also true.

I remember experiencing and displaying a few of these signs myself. Some that were strong for me were thinking of myself and my body as repulsive, dirty, or bad. I compensated for this feeling with the attention I got from perfecting my looks, but it didn't change my relationship with my body, which was mostly unhealthy. I remember feeling bad and guilty for what was happening to me, so I started to hide as much as possible.

Some other things that occurred because I experienced abuse as an older child, was exhibiting adult-like sexual behaviors, language, and knowledge. After abuse, I started experimenting sexually while I was still very young. I also started with self-injury in the form of wishing for death, drinking, and promiscuity. Some other very typical signs in teens and preteens include cutting, burning, and other non-suicidal self-injury. There can also be inadequate or hyperactive personal hygiene. All of these tend to give a child some misconstrued sense of control. Promiscuity also provides that sense of control, as in "I can get any person I want."

Lastly, the emotional toll of sexual abuse leads to depression, anxiety, suicide attempts, compulsive eating or dieting, fear of intimacy, rebellion, and running away from home. These are many of the most typical outcomes, but as you may know, this is a nuanced topic.

Unidentified and unattended sexual abuse can escalate, develop, and evolve in endless ways. The impact (and its effect) is equally predictable and unpredictable.

Below is the poem that I wrote about the shift that occurred in me from enduring sexual abuse, a shift that I wish someone had noticed and acted on. It has been an irreversible shift that I have learned to heal in a way that has allowed me to move forward much later in life than I would have hoped.

The Shift

Lost the child with ambition, happiness, and spark.
Now I had a secret.
The payment.
The cover up.

Then, I thought it would be just one time
but it happened again and again.

I didn't feel safe.

Lost trust.
Who could I turn to?
I felt so alone.

Started failing school.
Grounded.
They made me stay home, in a place I didn't feel safe.
Started drinking.
Started experiencing sexuality early.

I felt I had no one.

I barely remember school.
No direction.

All I cared about was finding attention from a boy.
Having a boyfriend.
Finding love.

I finally made it out but was full of scars.
Now how did I handle these scars?

Disrespecting myself.
Not knowing how to bond with others.
Drinking.
Putting myself in situations where I was abused by other men.

Life would spiral and I would lift myself out of the darkness.

I thought had I met the man I was going to marry
but he was verbally abusive
which was turning into physical abuse.

How did I cope? Drinking.

Today I know love and no longer drink to cope.

I still have my scars
but they are healing.
I learned to love myself first, fill my heart with my Higher
Power
and finally trust a man
...my husband.

I no longer have to cope.
I just have to heal.

5

The Damage Was Done

The darkest time of my life was the year filled with sexual trauma. I had a lot of bad years because of it, but during that time I was the most hopeless and helpless I have ever felt in my life. At the lowest point, I had made a suicide pact with a friend from school. I didn't want to be alive anymore. I didn't want to experience the pain anymore. During this time, I started failing school, fast. Everything in my life seemed to be falling apart and I had lost all desire to keep it together. I had very little drive and I just wanted to die because I thought it was the only way out.

Some of the worst pain I was struggling with was guilt and shame. Have you ever felt too shameful to face the truth or ask for help? I was so embarrassed to be in my situation that I couldn't bring myself to tell anyone. I felt trapped and abandoned. I felt lost and hopeless. I had sadness and anger eating away at me, but on the outside, I was sweet, pleasant, and outgoing.

I have always been a truly optimistic person. I get to enjoy that part of me now but during the years of having to deal with the men my mom was with, I was stifled. My sunny disposition was so suppressed that I forgot who I was—a being of love.

I knew that all I wanted was to love and be loved by my people and it seemed to get me in trouble. I wanted love back but not the kind of "love" I was getting. I wanted my mom to care for me. I wanted family time. I wanted the fairy tale family that got along and cared for each other. Instead, I received affection in all the wrong ways, and I hated it. I hated life. I don't even remember most of that time of my life because of the way I would disassociate from my reality just to survive it.

It felt like the walls were closing in at twelve years old. I should have been able to focus on school and sports. I wished my life was more about playing with my friends than trying to stay away from home and away from a predator. I was given more to think about than I ever asked for.

The way Richard was pursuing me and saying suggestive things made my skin crawl when I was around him. It caused me stomach aches and made me feel ill. There was a gut instinct that something was wrong with the whole situation. My intuition kept telling me something was being done to me. As far as I knew, he hadn't actually touched me since the movies and hadn't snuck and watched me shower since Hong Kong, but still my intuition told me something was wrong and I kept ignoring it and pushing it away, just trying to forget. I was overriding what my body was telling me—what I knew to be true.

I suffered through my nights, staying up as late as I could, wearing extra clothes to bed to protect myself. I suffered through my days, overtired, and wanting to end it all.

One night, it was confirmed that he was touching me in my sleep when I woke up with Richard in my room and his hand between my legs. His hand might as well have been around my neck because the panic I felt inside took my breath away. I completely froze.

That night, I tensed up and just rolled over to my side so I could close my legs. He knew I had woken up. With no exchange of words, he just got up and left. It was so terribly awkward and shameful.

Something irreversible happened when I woke up with Richard in my room that night. The clearest way I can explain it is that a part of me died. There was something in me that I couldn't recover: my innocence. I was so shaken by this experience that any ounce of safety I had felt was stripped away, and I became more vulnerable than ever. The fear and anguish consumed my entire being.

There are many times in my life I have ignored my intuition. Every time I have, there has been a price. Big or small, I am always reminded that my intuition is spot on and that I should trust and honor it. This is one of the biggest examples in my life. There is value in it, but just as much, if not more, pain in this lesson.

Have you ever ignored your intuition and later realized why you should have trusted it? Have you ever disregarded an urge or a nudge only to later find out it was your higher self guiding you in a safer direction? I want to encourage you to honor those urges and nudges. Honor those gut feelings as guidance toward your healthiest life and path of least resistance.

I know this now, but as a twelve-year-old, I did not have this knowledge or skill. I was just trying to survive my situation, and I had officially been broken by it. The next morning, I did my best to pretend everything was fine. Again. After staying up all night, I went to school and tried to make it through the day. I couldn't focus on anything in class, and after school, my mom could tell I was visibly distraught and asked me what was wrong.

She *finally* checked in on me and I was *finally* able to tell her. Something I had always wanted: my mother to focus on me, to *see* me. She saw how devastated I was, and I was able to share what happened with her. This was the first time it didn't involve screaming. Because she turned her attention to me and checked in, I was able to share truly and safely. I remember crying to her when I told her what had happened the night before.

Telling her was a very caring moment. She was listening to me. She wanted to help. There was hope. She was upset as well and agreed to figure something out. At the end of our conversation, she called a sex abuse hotline to get us help. They coached my mom, and she was ready to confront Richard about it. My mother was finally doing something about this mess. It was finally going to end. I was sure she was going to leave him.

After her call with the hotline, she headed into their bedroom to talk to him. I waited outside the bedroom for them to finish their conversation. When she came out of the bedroom, she said that Richard said I wanted it, and I screamed out at the top of my lungs, "I never wanted it!" Imagine that: a twelve-year-old child actually wanting to be pursued sexually by her stepfather. Unbelievable to most, right?

When I heard what he said there was a tightening in my throat and my heart sank into my stomach. I wanted to claw his eyes out. I couldn't even believe it. I was so enraged and equally paralyzed and unable to do anything about it. This was a nightmare.

How could she possibly believe that? How could it have turned out that way? I was sure my mom would know that was a lie. I was white-hot angry and filled with rage, disgust, and disappointment. The pain of my mother's betrayal was sharper than ever. The level of hopelessness I had reached was immeasurable.

His claim was such an outrageous, bold-faced lie that I figured would be the last straw for her. I thought we were going to finally leave but we didn't; my mom stayed. I could hardly believe it and yet, I wasn't surprised either. I cannot express the level of disappointment with my words as my heart cracked open and the pain felt like it would drown me.

I felt the hole in my heart widen, letting in more pain and anguish. Despair flooded over me when I realized we weren't going anywhere, and I would have to endure this life longer. More darkness crept in and more of *me* left. I don't know where she went, but I am sure as far from the situation as possible, leaving me there, empty, to deal with it all. I was struggling with a type of depression I had never reached before.

The solution to this situation was that Richard swore he would never do it again, and as far as I know, he never did—but that didn't really matter. The damage was done. I was gone. Being sexually abused had short-circuited my development in irreversible ways that caused great damage for the next thirty plus years.

Instead of leaving him, my mom put *me* into therapy. I shared what was going on at home with my therapist. I can only conclude that it was the times I grew up in but reporting the sexual, mental, and emotional abuse never went beyond our meetings. She didn't call any authorities to save me either, she just helped me navigate my thoughts about it. She listened, and I needed that. At the time, I guess I felt so hopeless that I didn't even expect my therapist to report it. We just talked. It did help to talk to someone, and I no longer wanted to end my life. Therapy helped put an end to my suicidal thoughts, but I was still stuck with my stepdad.

I was so far gone emotionally after this incident that to this day, I do not remember much of being thirteen, fourteen, or fifteen at home. I can tell you about school and friends and boyfriends but nothing about being at home. I recall studying for the SATs and going to school dances but my memories of being at that house are few and far between. Escaping reality of my home life became one of my top priorities.

Trying to stay away from him became even more difficult because not only did we *stay* with Richard, but we also moved into a new, better house to live with him longer. What I remember about moving was mostly just the new furniture, and I still hardly remember my time there. I think that my brain would only register the good things that I wanted to remember because the disappointment of staying with him was too hurtful. The only way to survive that level of pain was to disassociate from it.

During those years at the new house, both Richard and my mom drank more than ever. There was a lot of mental abuse leaving me always afraid, and I had no one to turn to, no guidance. The unpredictable nature of the household environment had me walking on eggshells. The sexual abuse had stopped but the damage was truly done. I was never the same innocent girl that just wanted to be loved and have the perfect life. I had lost all hope for that dream. I was at a stage of developing my own negative coping skills to combat the chaos of my everyday life.

Only in retrospect, can I understand why my mother may have not left her boyfriends and husband. I now see how she may have been afraid, dependent, and at risk. As an adult, I think of my mom at age twenty-four with a six-year-old being beaten by her boyfriend. I think if that were me, I would be petrified. I think of her at age thirty-one with a twelve-year-old being sexually harassed by her husband. I think if I were dependent on him, I wouldn't know what to do either. I realize now how she lacked strength, resolve, a healthy mindset, and financial freedom to keep me safe. However, these are no excuses for compromising the health, safety, and well-being of a child.

6

My First Addiction

Because I had lost all hope at home, I took matters into my own hands when it came to getting my needs met. I had mostly given up on my mother, but there was this part of me still trying to find some type of love, connection, and attention. In those middle school years, I was depressed and had low self-esteem. I felt worthless and gave up on the idea that I could get the love I wanted from my family. This is the age that I began to turn to boys at school for the attention I was missing.

As a result of the years of abuse and misconstrued displays of so-called love, I had no way of knowing how to bond. I didn't know about appropriate love. My mind had become sort of warped in how to get the attention that I thought I desired. I started using my looks, body, and sexual behavior to get the attention I so deeply craved. I had come to believe that sexual activity equaled love and love equaled sexual activity. I used what I knew to fill in the gaps in my life. I just wanted love so badly, and at that point, I would do anything to get it.

I had developed my first addiction: getting affection and attention.

I did not know it at that age but the one thing I was seeking was love for myself. As a result of enduring abuse, I didn't know how to love myself. I hadn't truly experienced love for myself; self-hatred was more familiar. Back then, I only knew how to sell myself to get the attention I wanted. By doing so, I sold myself short, and was therefore disrespected, so I hated and disrespected myself. It was a vicious cycle.

Even though I was getting the attention I thought I wanted, there was so much pain and loathing in being promiscuous. There is no depth to those empty acts of sex, and I felt hollow so much of the time. I always thought that if a boy was giving me that kind of attention, then he could love me, but I never felt truly loved or chosen.

Learning the power of sexual behavior at a young age gave me a sense of control. This can go differently for each person, and I used the behavior I was abused with to attempt to cope with my pain. I felt as long as I was in charge, I wasn't being abused. I started to behave this way sexually and with alcohol. I began drinking *so that* I could continue to behave promiscuously.

Having boyfriends pretty young, drinking, and staying out late was never alarming to my alcoholic mother, if she even noticed them, because she had the same coping mechanisms.

Rather, I had the same ones as her.

I drank to cope with my problems, and over time, my drinking became problematic.

My personal story of sexual trauma went on for decades, but I tell it now to create awareness around the impact of sexual abuse on children. When that fantasy of the perfect childhood and having love, guidance, and safety is shattered, so is that child. The children are tasked with trying to figure out what healthy love really looks like on their own.

Sexual abuse is something most people don't want to talk about, but according to Lauren's Kids, an organization dedicated to helping prevent child abuse along with helping survivors heal, one in three girls and one in five boys is sexually abused. The numbers are staggering. When this is happening, particularly to a young person, they feel alone. Because it often happens by the people they trust, they believe that they can't tell anyone. They fear the risk of destroying the family that they have, even if it is a dysfunctional one. They fear not being believed. They fear rejection for destroying the group cohesion. They may have been threatened with the secret, which adds even greater fear to a child. Fear of causing that kind of turmoil within the family can have an equally negative impact on the child as the abuse they are experiencing. This may happen with the same feelings in a community of some kind, whether religious, athletic, or club-community because those people become like family to them. Consider the travel sports teams and the amount of time they spend together going to tournaments and practically eating, sleeping, and living together during a season. A young person who is being perpetrated or pursued by a trusted parent or coach may be afraid to tell what is going on in fear of disrupting the team family that has gotten so close—in fear of becoming the outsider if no one believes them.

The perpetrators they trust are also teaching them distorted views of intimacy, relationships, and even love. They learn that "love" is dirty or perverse or secretive, and that is what they begin to believe. This can completely distort a child's sense of reality in many ways including the areas of love, sex, affection, relationship, communication, self-worth, intimacy, and more. This is why it is so important to have healthy and open conversations with our children about appropriate touches, personal space, and how to speak up when they need help. It needs to be a normal part of conversation, very much like the "stranger danger." This is also an opportunity for adults to learn about sexual abuse and educate others on how to spot it, intervene, and, hopefully, prevent it. Sometimes, adults will recognize remnants from their own past that they begin to question. The sooner an intervention or discovery/uncovering of sexual abuse or harassment is made, the greater chance for full recovery.

I value talking about this because I want to change how people think about the young person who is disrespecting themselves or spiraling in life. We must learn to recognize the signs as I've mentioned (but there may be more). Don't judge them; help them.

Look at a young teen who is acting out sexually and ask yourself, "Why would that young person do that?" Look at the high school scholar who suddenly becomes withdrawn. Look at the wild shifts in moods, appearance, behavior, and friend groups. They may show signs and need an intervention.

This acting out can even occur in adults who have never healed from the trauma of their past. Just because someone is of an age to be having sex, drinking alcohol, driving, and so on, doesn't qualify them to make healthy, responsible choices. We must look out for each other and step in to support when we can. Gone are the days where we sit idly by with the none-of-my-business belief.

The blessing of this situation is that anyone can move past it. As I shared in my poem, "The Shift," there is another side to this tragedy. We can create clarity from the chaos that life has brought. We can see the signs and break the cycles of generational trauma.

Addiction in its many forms is a textbook sign for trauma and unhealed wounds. It can show up in many ways, but a basis for catching it is seeing someone go to extremes or over-indulging. Many people suffering as I did start an activity, whether drinking or sexually acting out, to help numb the feelings of worthlessness, guilt, and shame, but over time, those mechanisms go from helpful to full-blown addiction. This bleeds over into other areas too, like addiction to food, gambling, shopping, or even exercising. It is when we use these tactics to fill the void in our heart that it becomes a true problem.

7

My Second Addiction

In many areas of my life, I developed the pattern of leaving one thing for another. I did this in relationships, careers, living situations, and more. I would begin to get uncomfortable in one situation and find my escape route to the next. I consistently ran from something or someone and ran right to the next thing that I figured would solve my current problem. My constant companion and bridge to courage was alcohol. My drinking helped me avoid myself. My actions, I believed, were helping me to socialize, to loosen up, to relax after a rough day, to destress, to have courage to speak, to fire me up for a confrontation, and many, many other "reasons," but the thing is, there's a tipping point.

Many who have substance use disorder—specifically in my case, alcohol use disorder—begin using a substance which truly aids in "taking the edge off" of whatever situation. But it's a gradual slippery slope. Where one drink may have helped in January, by March, it's two. The cycle continues. For some people, it's a shift from beer to liquor. For some, it's a shift from alcohol to another substance or action. For me, it was a steady increase of alcohol consumption. Did I realize I was in the throes of a full-blown addiction? Absolutely not, because our society has made drinking an acceptable and accessible outlet to all situations. Something to celebrate? Let's have a drink. Need to vent over stressors? Let's have a drink. Just completed a marathon? There's beer at the finish line! There is hardly a situation or culture where alcohol is frowned upon. More likely than not, it's encouraged!

I used alcohol to dull the intense feelings I had, and to help me get through situations. While I didn't know it at the time, it perpetuated the chaotic life I had grown up in. It kept me dull, cloudy, and foggy. It kept me walking through my own life in a daze. It was my constant companion, the one thing I could always rely on, and a part of my daily life, even when I was changing from one life to another.

No matter how many times I tried to start over, the real problem was the common denominator in all of this: me.

I wouldn't exactly say that I *was* the problem, but it would be safe to say I *had* a problem. I had a drinking problem that was destroying my life, relationships, and potential. Over time, alcohol seemed to cause the very problems I was trying to escape.

I had a predictable pattern of being in a relationship, job, or situation, and slowly starting to drink more and more to cope with the chaos. Sometimes this included partying harder, more consistently, or longer, and trying drugs. Sometimes it included mental, emotional, sexual, and physical abuse, and it always included terrible hangovers, which surprisingly, did not deter me from doing it again.

In order to deal with it all, my consumption escalated. It happened subtly, but then suddenly, the world around me represented the elevation of my drinking. The evidence was all around me. The quality of life was awful. Whether it was the arguing and fighting or the constant partying, the stress and despair became unbearable. Once I reached my limit, I wanted out.

My solution was to simply pack up and move. Sometimes, it was as quick as the next day. Other times, it would take months. Every time, I would leave and head for something—anything—more promising; except the promise of a new beginning wouldn't last long because I quickly found the party scene in my next situation and was right back in my pattern. I never had the intention of falling back into that lifestyle, but it happened again and again. I know now that it wasn't *because* of any situation I put myself in, but that the addiction was in me.

No matter where I ran, I couldn't outrun my addiction. I couldn't put a stop to my negative coping mechanism because it was all I knew. Drinking every night made sense to me. Toxic relationships, oddly, felt comfortable. They were familiar. Flirting to get what I needed or wanted made sense to me. So, when all else failed, I would leave to get a fresh start, but I simply restarted the pattern and always fell back into what I knew. Again.

The pattern was so often triggered by not getting the attention (my first addiction) I wanted in my current relationship. If I felt ignored, neglected, or not cared for, I would start seeking attention outside of the relationship. When I started to feel insecure in a relationship, my instinct to protect myself would kick in. It was urgent to get out before I got hurt. I believed I needed to hurt them *before* they could hurt me.

I would flirt and go out with other men to distract myself from the pain in my heart. I always had the hope of finding a man that I could finally rely on, someone that I could finally trust. I never had it growing up but there was a part of me that always held onto the dream.

Sometimes dating outside of my relationship would work, but it always complicated my life, which escalated my drinking to the point that the chaos became consuming. This is when I would become overwhelmed, decide yet again that I was done with it all, pack up, and move on. My pattern was to leave the old boyfriend for a new one, thinking he had more to offer. I was always after a better life, but with my own unhealed trauma, I was simply trading out one mess for another. I couldn't seem to leave the trauma behind.

I did this for decades, over and over, and it ran me ragged. I was a shell of a woman with very little hope or optimism about ever truly being happy. I was deeply depressed and always trying to cover it up.

I would never stop trying for a better life, but I am not sure I trusted myself to ever get there. I was surviving, dodging, and moving on; trying to escape my reality and always trying to numb the pain I was struggling with.

What was interesting about this is that no one would have ever guessed how bad it was. I was always in a relationship, I had good jobs, I had a place to live, I kept myself together, and I had gotten through school. On paper, I looked like I was doing just fine. There was nothing alarming about my day-to-day life from the outside looking in. It was the behind-the-scenes experience, my inner turmoil, that was so chaotic, but because I was able to keep up the facade, I even had myself convinced that nothing was wrong.

It was just a few drinks. It was just a night out. It was just wine with lunch. It was just a glass with dinner. I was always drinking, but I wasn't concerned. I didn't think I had a problem. I would compare myself to my mom, her boyfriends, family members, or other people I knew who always drank way more than me. My mom would pass out every night from drinking and I wasn't like that. I didn't hide vodka in my desk drawer. I knew of people way worse off who couldn't keep a job or get their life together and I was not like them. I was working, and later in life, I was taking care of children, I was giving back to my community. I was active; therefore, I did not identify as an alcoholic, and I wouldn't listen when others told me I needed to stop or slow down.

PART 2

What Drove Me to Drink

8

The Symptom vs. The Source

My addiction to alcohol was certainly a problem but it wasn't *the* problem. I was drinking to numb and suppress pain that lived so deeply in me that even the alcohol couldn't reach it. The depth of sadness I had from growing up in such a dysfunctional environment and all the traumas of that upbringing were so ingrained that I had no idea about how to alleviate that pain.

There are many people walking around with the unhealed pain of trauma with no idea that it is causing pain and negative coping behaviors. Societally speaking, we have not been given sufficient education, support, or tools to heal or manage pain. Many people don't feel like the childhood they had was particularly traumatic. It seems commonplace to hear stories of how rough a person's parents were, how strict, or how hot-headed a dad was. For generations, we have excused behaviors that currently are revealing evidence of having deeply harmed the very psyche of adults everywhere. The emotional absence of parents during a child's formative years deeply wounds so many. We know that now. Trauma comes in all shapes and sizes, and we cannot judge another's trauma.

For me, the guilt and shame of sexual abuse in my childhood was too much to bear. For most of my life, I felt like I had done something wrong. From the ages of sixteen to twenty-six, I wouldn't have said "I am drinking to numb the pain and sorrow of my upbringing," but that is certainly what I was doing. I was caught in each different circumstance and triggered to drink by the things and people right in front of me at those times. I struggled with triggers and their associated feelings for decades and still do from time to time. We may heal the wound but there is still a scar.

Do you have a real scar on your body? Sometimes if you bump it or scratch it, it can spark a similar pain to its original wound. That is how I feel about triggers in my later adult years. A thought, reminder, sound, or smell can take me right back to a traumatizing memory that I thought I addressed and healed. Before choosing sobriety, I chose the chaos of numbing the pain with alcohol. I tried to forget by blacking out, or at least fogging up my mind and that is what people saw: my addiction, not my pain.

Before I learned I could use alcohol this way, I struggled with suicidal thoughts, sadness, and anger. As a very young girl, I remember living in such confusion and fear. I used to wonder what I ever did for all these things to be happening to me. *Why was I chosen?* I figured I must have done something to deserve or cause this. I wondered if I had sent a message or given my abusers some feeling that that's what I wanted. I felt that way when Richard told my mom that I knew he had touched me in my sleep and that I wanted it. As wrong as it felt to hear him say that, it made me wonder and doubt myself. *Was I okay with it? Did I ask for it? Did I do something to cause this?*

I was forever changed that day at the movie theater in 1981. The little girl filled with joy, hope, and big dreams began to feel lost, lose respect for herself, and question what love was. I felt isolated and angry. This is where I changed to a point of no return. The sweet girl was gone. I had become a victim, and without understanding the dynamics of that, I fell right into the negative coping mechanisms of drinking, drugs, and dating.

As a nineteen-year-old, I loved it because I would go to the clubs and escape from everything. It was like euphoria being in the club, on ecstasy, and dancing my thoughts away. Being at the club was an escape. When I danced, I mentally went to a different place. For even a brief time, it felt like my reality and my problems didn't exist. It was like I was the only person in the room when I danced but it was also like I was putting on a show. I felt sensual and attractive as I danced and I got more of the attention I was hoping for from men. I was surviving and spiraling in that pattern, but this gave me some sense of control, albeit false.

There was an illusion of control and fun, but this was a hard time in my life because I started drinking a lot and I had begun experimenting with drugs. New people were coming into my life who also did drugs. It's true you are just like the people you surround yourself with. I started using ecstasy, and it was a relief just to be nowhere in this world.

Soon enough, it wasn't fun anymore. I was surrounded by people selling and doing drugs and every night was a party. I had moved to Houston, was working at a restaurant, and completely immersed myself in the party scene. I was trying to escape all of what I had been through, but at this point, I was traumatizing myself by putting myself in situations that were not safe, yet again, but it was the only scene I knew. Because my nervous system was so dysregulated, actually feeling unsafe and fearful was familiar. How messed up does that sound?

I ended up in situations that I regret. I ended up sexually abused in my late teens and early twenties because of the crowd I was hanging out with and how intoxicated, checked out, and black-out drunk I would get. I was with people and circumstances that I had to emotionally deal with for years. I just kept going deeper down the rabbit hole. Life went on like that for a while, filled with drugs and partying. I moved into an apartment complex and everyone around me was doing drugs, and I was even dating someone who sold drugs. I became rebellious and careless.

I was walking down this path with reckless abandon until I was stopped dead in my tracks one day. I was partying like any other day, and I was walking down the stairs by the pool. As I got to the bottom of the stairs, I caught a reflection of myself in a big window. My mouth fell open as I stood face to face with myself. At first glance, I saw my mom. It was my reflection, but I saw her so clearly that it felt like she was right there in front of me. It took my breath away and it sobered me right up. I knew at that moment, I had to get away from this lifestyle or I was going to turn into my mom.

That was it for me.

The very next day, I moved out. I refused to become like my mother. There was no way I wanted to follow in her footsteps, so I went to my grandmother's to get away. I needed a reset, and I needed a new plan. I desired a better path, so I decided to go to Blinn Junior College. I finally felt ready to make a change for the better. I was ready to leave the drugs and the partying behind. I applied, got accepted, and got started on a new future. I had my own dorm room with a roommate. I had a schedule in college, and I was going to make something of myself. I swore to put my past behind me, but my new ambition didn't last long.

I started school at Blinn Junior College. I tried to go to classes. I tried to do what was right, but I didn't know how to focus so I began to fall right back into the party scene again. I know now that my learning to focus as a child was impossible because I was on high alert. I lived in the dysregulated state of hyperarousal, always wondering what was going to happen next. In college, my lack of focus made me feel like a failure, like I would never make it as a student, and that led to the self-perpetuating cycle of thinking, *I'm no good at this so I'll just do what I know I can do well.* Discomfort led to overwhelm, and soon, I was back at my old habits. I stopped going to classes, I started hanging out with groups that partied, and I escaped all the time.

I failed that semester. I got an incomplete in all my classes because I didn't go to anything after the first couple of weeks. I flunked out and went back home to live with my grandparents and tried to figure out my next move.

I decided to try San Jacinto College. It was the same. I couldn't focus, I had no direction, and I didn't know what I wanted to do. Moving didn't work. Escaping didn't work. Nothing did. I quickly dropped out again and even tried Blinn again. I told my grandparents that maybe if I had my own private dorm room that it would be different. I couldn't get along with my roommate, so maybe if I was on my own *then* I could do it. The same cycle happened again. Again, it wasn't my fault.

It was repulsively predictable. I was so ashamed and upset. I couldn't figure myself out, which drove my drinking and escapism. I wanted the struggle to end so badly. I wanted to get out of this pattern, and yet, I felt like I had no control. I started each new situation with such big aspirations, but everything fell apart quickly. Soon enough, I would be trying to figure out my next move.

At this point, I thought I would never do anything with my life. I had fallen deeper into despair when my grandmother took me for some testing to find out what my interests were and what my passion was. I took a number of tests and as a result, I found that my passion was in the creative world. The tests determined that a smaller school would be good for me. This is when we discovered The Art Institute and things started looking up. I decided to take a music and video program. I was excited to pursue a creative career in film and entertainment. I started to visualize a future of fame, or at least working with famous people. This inspired and excited me.

I was eager to have a new light of hope, but I was also still partying. One night I went to the club where they were having nickel beer night. I have no idea how many beers I drank but at that price, I can tell you it was more than I needed, and it was certainly too many to drive.

I went out with a friend who lived in my grandparents' neighborhood. We told our families that we were going to the movies and ended up drinking nickel beers through the night. By the time we were ready to go home, I was black-out drunk and couldn't be reasoned with. My friend tried to take the keys away from me, but I of course thought I could drive.

I didn't listen, I drove, and I ended up getting a DUI. I can't tell you all the details of that traffic stop because I have zero memory. I was nineteen, thinking I was about to get my life together, and instead, what I got was a huge penalty for driving under the influence.

It was a big wake-up call for me. This cost me so much: in fees, of course, but also hope. That DUI took the wind right out of my sails. I beat myself up thinking that if I had moved somewhere new and started a new chapter that things would be different, but they weren't. I was screwed. I had to ride my bike to school that year because my driver's license was revoked. I was stranded in more ways than one and felt so stuck in my life.

It was mandated that I had to go to a 12-Step program. I forged most of the signatures required for my paperwork and penalties. I was also angry about getting busted. As far as I knew, everyone drank and drove. I figured this could've happened to anyone. I just happened to be the one that got caught.

This fueled the anger and sadness in me and further escalated my cycle of alcoholism. I was still in the club scene, trying to escape my depressing reality. The signs were apparent that my drinking was out of control. As if it couldn't get any worse, I went out again one night and the bar got raided. I ended up getting a public intoxication violation and the weight of my misfortune sunk me even lower. I could hardly handle it anymore.

I was fighting to get my life together academically and simultaneously sabotaging it with my addiction. I felt like I was in a losing battle of tug-of-war with myself and couldn't seem to find relief. It seemed like every time I found a sliver of hope, those dreams were dashed with despair.

9

Looking for Love in All the Wrong Places

I was thrown into another year of despair when my father died. I was only twenty. He was never around while I was growing up but that didn't mean I didn't wish for my father's presence and love. Particularly because of how terrible my mother's relationships were, I wished I had a true father figure I could rely on for support and saving. A protector. A champion for me.

I remember crying when I was very little, living with my grandparents, wondering why my dad never wanted to be around me. I felt abandoned by him too. No man I knew modeled what I understood it meant to be a real, kind, and true man. My grandfather was the closest I ever had to that, but he wasn't perfect. He had an explosive temper and it left me feeling fearful most of the time (add that to my childhood trauma). Our family had its struggles.

I didn't even have any positive male role models to look up to at school or in my community, making my relationships with boys, then men, very complicated. I can honestly say I had consistently toxic relationships with males altogether. Imagine the chaotic and twisted beliefs that had become a part of my childhood: absent dad, present perverted stepdad, early abuser who impacted my life significantly, granddad who provided for me, but who was unpredictable, and so on. My thoughts and beliefs about men and relationships were essentially twisted. I was on the road to great pain as I learned to navigate my way in the dark.

My father and I attempted to have a relationship while I was in high school. We tried to bond, but it was very hard. Neither of us had communication skills. He was living in Austin, Texas and I went to visit him from Houston. It felt very forced, but it seemed it was the only way to have a dad. Unfortunately, it didn't feel much better than any of my mom's boyfriends. My father was an alcoholic and delusional at times, always criticizing and assuming I was an impressionable teenager.

During my last visit with my dad, he accused me of shooting up drugs, which I had never done. He had seen a mole I have on the inside of my arm and immediately turned it into something else. I couldn't believe what I was hearing, and he wouldn't believe my explanation. It felt so hurtful, especially coming from a man who was an alcoholic and did drugs himself. I thought he had lost his mind.

His reaction to his inaccurate accusation ended our relationship, at least for me. I wanted nothing to do with him. I left that day without settling the argument and called my mom. I told her all about it and thank goodness she believed me. I was so distraught by his assumption but felt relief that my mom knew I wouldn't do that. I left for good that day and we stopped talking. I had no further intentions of forcing a relationship with my father.

Never having a positive male figure in my life messed with my understanding of love and connection in general. I didn't understand how to bond with people. I believe it also had a lot to do with moving and switching schools so often because people seemed interchangeable to me. The lack of connection to a healthy adult male followed me for the better part of my life. Because my mom showed me unhealthy relationships, specifically to prioritize the boyfriend over even family, I had no healthy idea of boundaries, no blueprint to turn to when I was confused, and I replaced boyfriend after boyfriend with the same versions of the one before.

This became true with friendships too, and because of this I went through both friends and boyfriends rather quickly.

I jumped straight into relationships. The pattern was there. It started well; we were going out, having fun, getting to know each other, and growing together. I fell in love fast and hard because I was so interested in a relationship helping me feel the love I was missing, the love I never truly felt. I was so willing for them all to be "the one" and it was easy to believe that in the beginning.

Soon enough, there were troubles. The relationship would develop, and I would notice things I didn't like and would try to change my boyfriend. I thought they were broken, and I could help. It couldn't be me, right? I was always trying to fix the guy I was with, but this always turned into a nightmare. I believed I could change them for the better. If I couldn't, I felt like a failure.

All my relationships were very volatile. It was all I watched growing up, so I figured this was what a relationship was: huge blow-ups followed by the make-up. This became the whole relationship. I always fought to keep relationships, even if they were bad. It was a part of the cycle. I expected it. I created it because it was all I understood about relationships. I did all I could to keep the relationships together, but there was endless fighting and screaming.

Every one of my relationships were filled with dysfunction, including physical and mental abuse. I stayed until I felt like I couldn't do it anymore. I eventually arrived at a point where something would click in me, and I would mentally decide I was done.

But when I decided I was done, I wouldn't leave. I would stay in the relationship feeling anger and resentment. Then, my drinking escalated. My boyfriends always asked me to stop drinking which made me so angry. I never thought drinking was an issue. I saw what was wrong with them, but they couldn't see it. The fighting continued, and my drinking continued. This is when I predictably started feeling like I was not getting the attention I wanted from that boyfriend. I can say *boyfriend* without putting in any particular name because this cycle was so repetitive with each guy I was with, it didn't matter who I was dating at the time. I went from one right to the next because when I wasn't getting the attention I wanted, I started to look outside the relationship for it. I forced the relationships to end without ever trying to work on them, without ever admitting problems and trying to work on myself.

I traded boyfriends like people traded baseball cards. I didn't care deeply about the boy; I was looking for the value. It wasn't even about sex or sexuality; I was trying to fill a void that was put there by my parents. I wanted to feel liked and loved. I wanted to be seen, believed, and heard. I wanted to be valued, and if I didn't get those things, I moved on and found a way to make it *his* fault. *I was a victim.*

By the time I made my move out of the relationship, I knew I was the victim. I would build it up in my head to justify leaving one guy for another and soon enough, I would break it off and move on. Each new man was a bridge to walk away from the last one. Because I never filled that parental void and never addressed, much less healed, the traumatic wounds instilled early on, this pattern carried over into my adulthood. When my life got too out of control, I just looked to create a new life by packing up and moving—kind of like a reset.

This happened time and time again, and while I had many boyfriends over the years, I never felt a deep sense of love or connection with them. I called it *love* at the time, but it was never love. I wanted something from a relationship that no boy or man could give me, but that never stopped me from trying to find what I was looking for from someone else.

As I got older, in college and the workforce, this behavior continued. I knew how to use my looks to get my way. I was hoping to find what I wanted *in* a man but was also fine just getting what I wanted *from* them. I loved the attention I got from men. There were many times in my life that I was trying to find and create my way and men would make their moves on me. It was thrilling to a part of me, yet there was another part of me, the little girl, who would get activated and irritated wondering what I was doing that would make men feel like they could treat me this way. *Was I asking for it?* I was sure all any man ever wanted was sex. I loved the power and false sense of control it gave me. See the paradox?

This led me to more drinking. I drank *so that* I could behave that way. *So that* I could survive my situations. *So that* I could continue on in my life without losing my sanity. These years of my life were so challenging, and yet, I had mastered that facade. From the outside, people thought I was fine because I had always been an incredibly capable woman. I made everything look good on the outside while falling apart on the inside.

I was stumbling through my many attempts at college, struggling with relationships, and drinking seven nights a week. Depending on the night, I was either partying until dawn or it was just chardonnay before bed. No matter how much, I was drinking every day. I was working serving jobs and just barely making it financially. No matter how much I ever wanted to get ahead, I always seemed to fall back into the party scene. I never considered myself an alcoholic. I thought I had it under control. It didn't feel extreme. I felt as long as things appeared in order, I had it together. It didn't *interfere* with my daily life; it *was* my daily life.

My father died during my last year at The Art Institute, over a year since that last argument. While I didn't recognize it then, Spirit helped me reconnect before his death.

A friend of mine wanted to go to Austin for a trip and I offered to take her. I told her that I wanted to drop by my dad's house, and she was fine with that. When I went to his apartment, a woman answered the door, and she said my father was in the hospital. It seemed so crazy to me that my relationship with my father was so strained that I wouldn't have even been told he was in the hospital. I left the apartment walking very slowly, thinking about the craziness of my life. It was like I was detached, simply observing my own life. I know now that this detachment is a natural protection mechanism which develops in those who have had great trauma.

I remember my visit to the hospital so vividly. The first thing I noticed when I walked into his room was that he was hooked up to blood-filled tubes from machines. This made my stomach turn. I was concerned for him. I felt nervous about it all, and I could feel my heartbeat in my face. All my life, I wanted a father—*my father*. I had been chasing boys for this man's love and now, I was faced with his mortality. It didn't matter how much we had disagreed or argued, I wanted my daddy.

Over the next few days, I did everything I could to earn quality time. I brought him gifts to his room. I visited as much as I could. I was so scared, but he told me he would be okay. Everyone kept telling me that he would be okay, so I went back home to Houston.

A week later, very early in the morning, I received a call from my Aunt Margo, and she told me that my dad had died. I drank the whole night before, so I had an excruciating headache and when she told me, I fell apart. All I can remember was sobbing. I felt like those tears were coming from the depth of my soul from two decades of abandonment with no chance of redemption. I knew I had lost all opportunity to have a relationship with my father and this was absolutely devastating to me. I was so thankful to get to see him one last time, but his death woke me up to the fact that we had missed so many opportunities to bond with each other.

I remember the sadness, but there were waves of anger that came over me, too. I was the victim again! Realizing no one told me he was sick and hospitalized made me question his whole side of the family. Then, not finding out he passed as soon as he did, sent me over a new edge. I felt alone, abandoned, stranded, and completely invisible. The pain became insurmountable.

I knew I had always wanted his love and there was officially no hope for that now. This broke me down to the core, and that became one of the most challenging years of my life.

Looking back, I realize I was nudged to go and see him that day. Something told me to go. Of the countless times I ignored intuition, listening to and following that feeling paid off. Ignoring it and not getting to see him would have completely broken me.

Following his death, I became even more vulnerable. I felt destroyed and couldn't keep up my facade. I was at an all-time low. A boyfriend from my high school years had come back into my life, and he was a bad influence on me (still seeing myself as victim). I told myself I would never let him back in my life but with my guard down,

I let him right in. I think that I didn't want to be alone in my grief and he showed up right in that window.

He insisted on going with me to Austin to dad's funeral. We fought on the way, and he made the day and the argument all about him, which delayed us, causing us to miss part of the service. It was a horrible day, and I was spiraling.

That day became a trend for the rest of the year.

I was the most self-destructive the year after my father died. I moved to a new apartment and the guy ended up living with me. My drinking was at an all-time high, and I was trying to escape everything. I had no sense of control over the way things were going and I missed my dad so much. There was something hopeless about my life knowing he was really gone, knowing I would never have a relationship with him. Deep within, it signified something much greater that I wouldn't figure out until much later.

Shortly after his death, I received some money from his passing, so I was able to buy a car, pay off my school loan, and afford the apartment. This was a relief, but the money went fast. The boyfriend never contributed to anything; in fact, he was stealing from me, and he was drinking heavily, doing drugs, and mistreating me. Victim.

When I looked at my life, I felt like I had gone backwards. I was in yet another terrible relationship, partying to the verge of insanity, feeling lost, confused, and without love once again. I was just going day-to-day, mostly trying to numb my pain.

10

Finally Finding My Way Through School

I was slow to recover after my dad died, repeating the same destructive cycles, and deep down knowing I felt lost, untethered, and aimless, but my time at The Art Institute miraculously held me together and kept me going. It was the light in my life. Going to school somewhere I was passionate about kept me going through some of my darkest days. I was glad to finally be on a path to my future, and with my graduation within my sights, it was the glimmer of a possible future.

Another bright spot in my days was living in Montrose, which was a very artsy area in Houston. This is a time when gay men populated specific areas to create a safe, tight-knit communities. Montrose was one of those areas, and I was lucky enough to have been a part of this group. I remember the safety and relief I felt living and going to school there. It was such a change for me—feeling safe.

I was the most myself at that time because I was around guys who weren't trying to have sex with me all the time. I had friends. I had people around me who didn't want something from me. I didn't feel any pressure from them, and I was able to relax a bit. This was a first for me. I had a group of friends who accepted me as-is.

College is a blur because of the way I lived. I wonder sometimes how I made it through, as I lived such a chaotic lifestyle, self-destruction was high, and so was I. One of the things that I thought I needed to do was flirt with my professors. I figured that if the teacher liked me, then he'd give me a good grade. I remember being in class, trying to get attention. I spent more time figuring out how to get the grades instead of owning my education and putting in the work.

I think back about how different things might have been had I taken more responsibility for what was driving me.

I graduated in 1992. I did it. I graduated from college. I walked across the stage and received a degree. I was on my path. It is one of the most positive memories I have from that phase of my life. I'll never forget my graduation night.

My mom and her new husband were there at the ceremony, and I, once again, thought that he was wonderful. I was very happy for her, and despite everything, I truly wanted her happy.

I felt like I was shining that night at a celebration dinner, surrounded by the people who were the most important to me: my aunts, grandparents, mom, and friends. I was finally proud of myself, and I felt like everyone around me was proud of me, too.

That night, my grandfather and I danced to "Unforgettable" by Nat King Cole. He was the only man that never tried to touch me. He was the only man I truly felt I could trust. He was the most reliable man in my life, and it felt so special to share that dance with him. That will forever be one of my favorite memories.

11

Finding My Passion and Career

I got my start in television very young and other than my time raising children, I have worked in the industry for all my adult life. I have a true passion for the pace and energy of television, and I am pretty darn good at it. I have always been good at it *because* of my love for it.

I could say this work is *in* me because even during some of the most challenging times of my personal life, I still thrived at work. I always got the positions and promotions I went for, and I advanced frequently. Some might say I was a tough and demanding boss, but I always got the job done and performed well under pressure. It was all a part of the environment where a mistake would be broadcasted in front of millions, and we had to be on our game or face public shame. I made my mistakes, but more often, I ran the show like I was born for it.

I started my path in television while still in college at my first internship in the promotions department at Paramount 20. It only lasted about a month long, and I was still working a server at a restaurant, but that short time lit my fire for the work and encouraged me to keep applying for new jobs in television. During that time, I was still partying and believed that all I had to offer was my looks.

Because of this, there was some flirtation between the director of promotions and me. It was just the two of us in the department. It was always that way with me. I would think to myself, *Maybe if he liked me, I could get a job there.* So, I entertained his advances and flirted back. I learned this tactic early and used it whenever I thought it would help me get where or what I wanted. I always used my bosses' crushes on me to my advantage.

It was what I learned in my youth: let inappropriate things happen, and you can get things you want. I got to go on my trip to Europe. I got to live with my grandparents. I got jobs or gifts. I always had a boyfriend because I accepted inappropriate behavior, but at least I was with someone. The trade-off of tolerating inappropriate behavior was that it got me what I wanted. I felt like I was in control. I learned that very young, used it for my survival, and it worked in my favor.

My internship ended, I finished school, and once I graduated, I ran the closed-circuit televised station at the greyhound racetrack in Galveston, Texas. This was the footage people saw on all the televisions in the building. Even though the public didn't see it on their TVs at home, it was still a rush to see my work broadcasted on *any* television.

During my time there, I had the chance to learn a lot and to experience many facets of live broadcast. For example, I was responsible for operating the cameras during races at the dog track. I was challenged with such things as maintaining the right distances and focus on the dogs for optimal viewing. While it gave me the excitement I needed to continue this path and provided an opportunity for me to improve my skills, I stepped away from it after seeing the treatment of the dogs. I view animals like children—innocent to the sometimes-evil ways of people. I just couldn't be a part of it.

While trying to make my way into the television industry in a more permanent way, I kept my serving job and my lifestyle. I was grateful for the job because it started later in the day. I could keep up with my partying at night, sleep into the late morning, and start work around four in the afternoon. This made room for hangovers before doing it all over again. It was a familiar cycle. Work, party, sleep, and back at it again. I wondered if I'd ever get out of it.

Unexpectedly, one day, my Aunt Melissa said she found a job she thought I'd be good at. It was in the traffic department at Liberty Sports Communications building daily logs for the network, Prime Sports Rocky Mountain. I was so grateful that she found and suggested the opportunity, and even more excited when I got an interview.

Even though I knew nothing about the job, I went in for the interview. The woman's name who interviewed me was Tammy. I'll never forget that during my interview she asked me the traditional, "What are your strengths and weaknesses?" question, and I naively admitted that I was not good about being on time. I did not get the job, yet oddly enough, something about me stuck with her; I did get a call from Tammy when they were hiring for contract work a few months later. I never thought I'd hear from her again, but I did. I was so excited. I would have a new chance to show her my capabilities, and that I could get to work on time, which I *mostly* did. I was ready for a new path in life.

12

My Third Addiction

I started at Liberty Sport Communications and the training began. Life was finally going to start for me. I was going to be all in. This was my chance. I was headed in the right direction, and I was so motivated about the prospect of a new life, *AGAIN*.

This was my third addiction: the promise of a fresh start.

It, too, was like a drug: the fresh scent of hope in the breeze when I would take off for a new life. It didn't matter what was next as long as it got me away from my last situation. I got high on the idea of escaping my past and could never get enough of these new chances. It was something I lived for and regularly looked forward to. Of course, I always wanted each new situation to work out and be the final one, but it never was. It was just a few weeks or months before that glimmer of hope faded and I was looking for my next out, but I was ready for *this* job to be the one.

I got through my training and got started with my work. Then one day, I saw a guy standing down the hall from my cubicle. Immediately, I had butterflies in my stomach. I just knew at that moment he was my soulmate. He was going to be part of my new beginning.

I was still with a boyfriend, but I didn't care. That was my cycle:

"all in" in a relationship, then things would go bad, I would be treated poorly, and of course, it was never my fault (this is what's called, living in the victim role). As soon as I could find a new man with potential, I would set my sights on him and go for it. Here I was, perpetuating my cycle.

I was excited about my new soulmate, James. We hit it off right away. I knew I had met the perfect guy. He didn't want to take advantage of me right away. He treated me with respect, a true gentleman. I had a great job and a new guy that I thought could love me and treat me right.

My current boyfriend found out I was cheating. I was sure that he was, too. We got into a huge fight about it, and it became physical. He lunged at me, and I grabbed a knife and cut his arm. We both knew we were terrible together and wouldn't admit it but hurting him crossed a line. Sure, it was self-defense, but we got to such a point of fighting that neither of us was safe with the other.

In countless situations, I went into fits of rage. I had great anger. There was unattended trauma from my past that got set off by the slightest offenses. This showed up in my career as well, but I was able to blame production breakdowns. In relationships, I found a reason for my rage, but the truth was, it was *in* me. The same way that trauma triggered the start of my drinking, my rage was just a symptom of a lot of unhealed wounds.

When we got into the physical fight that ended with my actually cutting him, I was so afraid I would go to jail. Our screaming matches had never gotten to that point, and I think it shocked both of us. A few days later, things calmed down and we simply ended it. I moved out into my own place.

It wasn't more than a week before James was basically living with me. I had never lived alone. There was always a guy that I ended up being with. I could not be alone with myself. I never wanted to be alone with my thoughts and feelings. It definitely fueled my drinking, but this strategy also put me into living situations that were forced, just to avoid myself.

Because I was trying to escape myself, I tried to be whoever I thought the person I was with wanted me to be. There I was, at twenty-five, starting over again. I was smack dab in the middle of my pattern of switching to a new man—starting over, taming my drinking, playing house, making dinners together, and having light-hearted fun. Every time I'd start over, I tapered or hid my drinking. I was always excited about a new beginning. I thought I was finally going to have the love and life I always wanted.

Another part of the pattern included running the narrative in my head that this guy was *the* guy. He was the gentleman that would finally treat me right and take care of me and make it all better. I would finally be better with *this* one. I convinced myself that I was happy and that we were going to live happily ever after.

Addiction is transferable. I know this now. If we do not address the addictive personality the addiction will just transfer from one focal point to another. Being so hungry for a new start was like putting a bandage over something that needed stitches. New starts, new men, and new jobs never solved my problems. They never resolved the anger in me.

The sign of an addictive personality is the fixation and overuse or over-indulgence of something. When we *must have* something for our life to work or to feel good about ourselves, then we are addicted to the illusion that our answers and worth lie outside of us. We must see this for what it is if we want any hope of a new life.

It's also important to identify the role of the victim in our relationships. Victimhood can become a part of our identity; it is a defense mechanism to cope from past trauma. And then it becomes a habit, a pattern, and a lifestyle. I blamed others for every negative thing that happened in my life. I lived in a victim mentality.

13

Climbing the Ladder

Despite my excessive drinking over the years, I somehow kept moving up in work. I never had confidence in myself, but no one could tell. There were so many times I didn't understand how I was able to move up the ranks. I used to look around and wonder, *How the hell is this happening?* I was always getting the job done, but behind the scenes, I was always drinking, angry, confused, and living life in a blur.

In retrospect, I wonder what would have been possible if I did not drink all those years. How far could I have gone if I was on my A-game? Being sober now, I am clear that I have skills, possess a gift, and bring light to my work. I cannot imagine where I would be if I would have been clear-headed for the majority of my career.

This brings me sadness from time to time but doing the healing work helps me forgive and release.

Some of those dark times included stumbling my way through my workdays sleep-deprived and hungover. I remember going into work with only three hours of sleep because I'd gone out the night before. I called in sick sometimes because I could not get out of bed. I was up against my own self-destruction. The guilt was unbearable, so I always ended up lifting myself out of bed and going into work late. Somehow, I always made it happen.

This was still too early in my career to ever consider that I was an alcoholic. I was too successful for that to cross my mind. True alcoholics couldn't hold a job, right? I had never known what it meant to be a *functioning* alcoholic, because I was raised by them. This was truly a normal thing for me. I just assumed that if I was successful, my drinking was under control. I always measured this by comparison. I simply made sure that I was nowhere near as bad as my mother.

James and I were together and happy. Things were flowing smoothly, then I got another break at work. The program manager for Prime Sports Rocky Mountain had an opening for an assistant and he personally selected me. I was surprised, honored, and yet again, wondering, *How is this happening?* I was so excited to be moving up and learning another part of the industry. I gladly took the position and got started full steam ahead.

Three short months into my new job, my boss took a leave of absence. He was sick and wasn't sure when he would return. I was thrown into his role of creating the schedules for Prime Sports Rocky Mountain yet had very little knowledge about what he did. I was equally nervous and determined to learn once he went on sick leave and I did. I had no idea what to do but I knew it was sink or swim time. I figured it out!

I dove in and learned from the Program Managers at the other networks around me. I was grateful they were willing to help and guide me. I think it was one of those signs from the other side that I am always taken care of because this was an extremely hard time for me. Trying to learn the job of the Program Manager and playing the role of assistant to myself was a daunting task that I didn't feel prepared for, but somehow, I made it work. This was all while still drinking after work regularly. No one suspected I was struggling. I have no idea how I kept going, but I did, and I did well.

I did my best in the position, but I wasn't given the job as manager. Another six short months later my boss did not return as he'd been diagnosed with a serious illness. This came as a surprise to me, and then we were faced with replacing him. Once the station was sure that he wasn't coming back, they posted the job. I assumed they'd give it to me.

I was distraught because I had done so much in his absence. I felt like my hard work and commitment was overlooked. I figured they were going to give the job to someone else after I had put so much effort into learning the position when they needed me. I was sure of it. I had to formally apply and after they interviewed multiple people, I got the job! I was now the official Program Manager for Prime Sports Rocky Mountain. Even though I knew nothing about sports, I had proven I could do the job, and I was excited to have it.

Eventually, I got to hire an assistant. I was still learning my job and was now having to teach someone else their job. I was able to do it, but I was not very nice at that time. I was very explosive and reactive under so much stress, just like in every other relationship I had.

I found out later that people were afraid to tell me there was a problem because I would get so mad. We were producing live TV so if there was a mistake, everyone would see it. I had a hard time with my anger. I was full of rage from my upbringing. Anger and rage were what I knew. I especially had a short temper with other people's excuses. I had a leadership style and mentality that intimidated people.

With all the stress from the job, I couldn't wait to get home and have a glass of wine, or two. My drinking increased a little bit at a time. That stress took a toll on my relationship with James as well. Soon enough, we started having problems and fighting a lot. No one seemed to understand what I was going through.

During my time as Program Manager, Fox came in and Liberty Sports and Fox Cable Group merged. All regional networks were now under the Fox umbrella, and they wanted to move the managers to their regional cities. That meant they wanted to move me to Denver, Colorado.

With the decline of my relationship, this felt like a perfect opportunity for me to start again. My alcohol use was escalating, and my pattern was set in motion, I found my next out for a new beginning... or so I thought.

14

Making a Run for It

Once again, I was ready for a move and a fresh start. I wanted to leave James and start a new life in Denver on my own. I entertained him and played along when he thought he was moving with me. I even took him to Denver to look for a place to live. I was going to break it off before I actually moved, but things did not go according to my plan.

James asked me to marry him on the trip to look at houses. We had gone to Breckenridge for a day, and he got down on one knee. I was shocked. It caught me by surprise, and I couldn't think quickly enough, so I said yes. Suddenly, I questioned my idea about leaving him. With this proposal, I thought the Universe had this plan for me, and I was supposed to follow it, but it wasn't what I wanted. Something in my body felt like this was not right. It simply wouldn't work, but I ignored it.

Nonetheless, we packed up and moved to Denver. We rented a house, and I started my new job. James did not have a job, so I was supporting us both. This was very frustrating to me because I grew up believing that it was the man's job to be the provider, and still wanting someone to take care of ME, not the other way around. I began to have even more resentment toward him. I was working and he seemed worthless. My anger and lack of patience was building.

He finally got a job selling copiers and I was relieved to again be a double-income household. All the while, the same cycle continued: work, drink, go to bed, and do it all over the next day.

Drinking wine after a long day at work was a part of my routine. It started as soon as I got home, pouring a glass just to relax. Then, it continued into a glass while cooking dinner and one with dinner. One glass turns into two glasses and before I knew it, I'd had my third—every day.

While growing up, I watched both my grandfather and my mom drink every day. It's just what people did. I didn't think much of the way it was affecting my life and work, just like it never occurred to me why my grandfather or my mom drank each day. I never considered that there were reasons people chose to make this a daily activity a hobby. I wasn't happy at home, so I drank. I was happy at work, so I celebrated. Things kept moving right along. We continued with the wedding planning, and we bought a house. All the while, I had a nagging almost guttural feeling that it wasn't right. We kept getting deeper into the mess. My escape was taking my dog on hikes every Saturday. I knew James would not go, so I had time alone. The whispers and feelings got stronger, but I was so weak.

I wanted to escape more than ever because the fighting had gotten bad. Again. It became physical and there was so much anger between the two of us that the fighting seemed endless. I felt like I was in too deep and couldn't get out. I was miserable, and I'm sure he was too. I started visualizing myself moving out on my own, yet we were still moving forward with the wedding.

The anger from James intensified and I had one foot out the door. I started seeing clear signs of the end for us, so I started looking outside of the relationship for attention. Again. The logic of this pattern was always to hurt them before they could hurt me or leave them before I was left. It was time to run so I began looking for a job in Los Angeles. I knew if I was going to rise in my career, I had to get to corporate, so I started planning my escape route.

I knew for sure I was leaving after my grandma came to visit and

James was cruel to me during her stay. I thought if he would treat me that way in front of my grandmother, then he had no limits. The final day we were together, we had gotten into a huge fight over something trite, meaningless.

Later that same day, we fought again—over a pen. That's right, a writing utensil. At that point, we fought about anything because the relationship was over. The fighting and the drinking had spiraled out of control. That day, I knew I couldn't do it anymore. I was done. I was deeply exhausted and angry.

It was six weeks before the wedding. I went to the garage to call my mom, and I told her I had to break off the wedding and she supported me. I went back inside to tell him it was over. He didn't fight me. It was finally over for the both of us.

Moving on from the relationship quickly, I decided I was going to start a new life in Los Angeles. In one month, I found a job with Fox, broke off the engagement, and sold my house. My mom came to Denver, we packed up my car, and made the drive to California together.

The road trip went well. I specifically remember making our way over and stopping in a dry town for the night. We searched high and low for alcohol because there was no way my mom or I could skip a night. We really did live and plan our days around drinking.

We made it all the way from Denver to the coast and got into a big fight as soon as we got to LA while we were trying to find an apartment. We triggered each other. She found a hotel to stay at and I stayed with my friends from Houston. At that point, I couldn't wait for her to leave. I know now that spending time with her showed me more of myself. Her presence acted as a mirror, and I did not like what I saw. I was crawling out of my skin. I couldn't wait for all the fighting to end and the people who *made* me miserable to be out of my life. I didn't realize it then, but I was always playing the victim and everyone else was at fault for my pain and suffering. Playing the victim was such a major part of my suffering that I felt like I had no control of life, but I was often the one who needed to take action and responsibility. I couldn't see it then, but I was completely wrapped up in the role.

I moved into a teeny-tiny loft and was feeling a bit sorry for myself. I thought, *What have I done? I'm in a new state, alone in LA with my dog, in an apartment with no bedroom.* I felt so low. I moved from a beautiful home to this: basically, a spare bedroom, filled with storage. I felt like such a mess, trying to figure out what was next. I just had to flip the script and remember that I was starting fresh and could create a new life!

To get to LA, I had to take a step down at work, but I knew I'd get ahead again. I started with a new network at Fox as a coordinator. In terms of career, I was right back in the swing of my pattern—the high of a fresh start. Nothing bogging me down. I had another beginning and lots of dreams. Despite all the chaos of my personal life, I knew how to navigate a fresh start, and I felt ready for it.

I made new friends and I started going out right away. It was like playtime. This was the first time in my adult life without a boyfriend or fiancé. I hadn't been single since high school. I felt free to do whatever I wanted in a new city. It *was* my chance to do what I wanted! I'll never forget going out with my girlfriends one of those first weekends and saying that guys are like candy, and I could pick any one I wanted.

I was trying to act strong, but I was so broken inside. I had shoved down the emotional hurt from failing with James and drowned it with alcohol. I had made so many huge life changes in such a short time that this breakup was getting the best of me. I had never gone as far as being engaged so this separation felt a bit different. Something else that felt different was that I left a man without knowing who was next. This was my first time being alone in a very long time and that terrified me. I drank to deal with some of that pain, but I also tried to shift my focus to work.

I see now that I was a runner and an avoider when it came to the things that deeply bothered me. I would leave physically by leaving the job or the man, or I would leave mentally by drinking myself gone. This behavior never solved my problems. In fact, it caused them to repeat.

Have you ever heard the phrase, "Wherever you go, there you are"? I could have moved around the world a dozen times, but I could never outrun or avoid my pain which then manifested in relationships or problems at work. The cycle *is* the sign, and it takes great courage to admit this. Courage I still didn't have.

15

Office Drama

I was excited to start this new job in LA; I had my hopes super high. It was a start-up network, so I was given multiple roles. There was a lot expected of me, but I was in no place to give it my all. I was in a constant state of clouded lethargy: hungover, exhausted, and brokenhearted. I struggled to find a groove.

To top it off, I felt like an outcast with the group. My new boss, Mark, rarely gave me the direction needed and was very physically and emotionally unavailable. There was a lot of office drama and trauma. Personal and professional lives got mixed up a lot in that office. I noticed that Mark was often in his office with the female program manager. It didn't seem hard to guess what might be going on.

What happened behind closed doors became apparent to me when I was in Mark's office one afternoon and I had a bad crick in my neck. He asked me what was wrong and when I told him, he said he could massage it out. He approached me and placed his hand, first on my arm, and ran it up my shoulder, and placed both hands on the back of my neck. As uncomfortable as I was, I allowed it to happen. I froze in discomfort the same way I had when I woke up to Richard's hand between my legs. I froze in fear and disgust. I was twelve years old again, and panic paralyzed me.

He was rubbing my neck, the door was closed, I could tell he was looking down my shirt, and I didn't stop it. I just waited. I can still feel the sensation of heat in my face and the pounding of my heart. It felt like an eternity that I had to wait for that to be over.

I left that office as quickly as I could, and I did what my mom always told me to do in my childhood: forget about it. Let it go. Move on. Well, I did. Life went on as usual and it was the only time something like that happened, thank goodness. I never spoke up. I never demanded an apology. I never stood up for myself.

I never liked that office but after that incident, I had my own proof and reasons. I didn't want to be in that kind of environment, not only where I was susceptible to sexual harassment, but also received little to no training to do the work. I was mostly floundering in everything going on but as usual, no one knew what I was going through personally. I successfully hid my heartbreak and drinking, which I still didn't identify as a problem.

The beginning of the end for my time at that network was the actual launch of the network. It was scheduled for New Year's Day, 2000. I had gone out on New Year's Eve with the intention of a glass or two of champagne. I knew I wanted to be home early because I had to be at the office the next day for the launch, which was a Saturday. I, of course, drank way more than I planned, and got home very early in the morning.

I didn't make the launch. From a deep sleep and a terrible hangover, I heard my phone ringing. I was already a couple of hours late. I was so sick, but I forced myself up and made it to the studio.

The entire day was a mess. There were multiple issues and I got blamed for all of them. The old station logos were not taken off the repurposed programming and our new logo did not cover it properly. There I was, the coordinator, and all these directors that were involved received no blame. I was an easy target. I was the weak link. I hadn't made it in on time, so I became the scapegoat.

I was scrutinized for multiple people's mistakes, and it was awful. I didn't know how to defend myself. I was paralyzed. There I was being taken advantage of, and I couldn't stand up for myself. Just like my mom could not stand up for me over and over. I had no boundaries, no understanding of boundaries, and no way to connect that to my childhood at the time. That week, I had executives from other departments in the company come up to me and apologize for their behavior. I was angry. I wanted to run away, quit, go back to Houston, but I didn't. Instead, I decided to lift my head up and find another job. It was time for yet another new start.

I started looking and found a job as On-Air Promotion Manager for FX Network. I had no experience, but I went for it. I knew I could learn and adapt. I had been doing it for a while and was finding my way. I didn't always have self-confidence, but I was always willing to give it a shot. The funny thing is, I got a very good recommendation from the last station when I let them know I was moving on.

One thing Mark told me that has always stuck with me was that I was acting like a cog in the wheel, and that I needed to be the entire wheel. He explained that we shouldn't just stop at knowing one little part of the process, we should know the whole picture. I wanted a better understanding of the whole network process. This encouraged me when going for this new, unfamiliar position.

Working this position boosted my confidence because I was seeing the whole wheel and wanted to learn and know more. I felt like I could do as well as anyone else and I could figure out a way through difficult situations.

As I grew in that position, I wanted to expand my knowledge of the business. By then, I had already experienced operations, programming, and on-air promotions, and within a year I was promoted to Director of On-Air Promotions and Scheduling. Each promotion felt easier and easier. My experience in other areas and knowledge of the business helped me to get the job.

Just because I did not have the on-air experience didn't mean I could not do it. Sometimes we think we can't go for something because we have not been trained in that area but that is not true. Learning more about a business or industry allows us to expand our knowledge and our worth. I took my experience and utilized it in my new position. I learned how to best promote the programming on air and to organize a broken area so that it functioned optimally.

I will never forget when the president of the company told me that I had a "fire in the belly." He told me, "That is something you can't learn, it's innate." That awakened something in me. This man saw me. He wasn't taking anything from me, he didn't want anything from me, but he saw me. He saw something I didn't have words for. I think I always felt the fire but never heard it explained that way before. Suddenly, I recognized the fire and it lit me up. I believe I learned to survive and because of that, I had built a fire in myself that burned high. I knew I was going to break free and make it no matter what.

During my time as director, I was challenged, and I thrived. It was another sink or swim situation. I worked hard, failed sometimes, and succeeded others, but I was on the track to becoming Vice President of On-Air Promotions. This was another wow moment for me to remember that I was once a girl with no direction, struggling aimlessly, and then I made my way to the Director of On-Air Promotions for FX Network and continued my climb in the company. It was a high point in my life.

I had done exactly what I said I was going to do: I had told myself I'd be a manager again in a year, and I did it.

16

Marriage and Kids

I was feeling unstoppable at this point in my career, and in life in general. I certainly wasn't looking to date anyone, as I was still recovering from the last breakup with the wedding cancellation. I just wanted to enjoy being on my own, but a few people at work informed me that a mystery man had begun an investigation on me.

He had people that worked for him trying to get information on me. He had never dated anyone from work before so apparently, he was being extra cautious. They were letting me know that someone was interested but wouldn't say who. They just wanted to find out about me for his sake. It was funny to me, so I played along. The mystery of it was fun and went on for a couple of weeks.

After all, it was a good distraction from my grief about my break-up, and it played into my familiar routine and addiction to attention. However, I had no intentions of dating someone from work. I met James at my job, and I had since sworn off dating co-workers, but then I got a call from Ray inviting me for a drink or dinner. I said no. I turned him down flatly.

He was a bit taken aback by this. I told him I wasn't going to date anyone from work again because I figured he knew my story. He paused on the other end of the phone for a moment.

"No, I don't know your story. I just thought we could go for a drink," he responded kindly.

It was then that I realized *he* was the guy I was waiting to hear from. He was who everyone was investigating me for. I actually thought I was waiting for a call from someone else, or at least, he was not on my radar. I was so glad he did not take no for an answer. I still didn't want to date anyone from work, but I agreed to dinner because I didn't want just a drink, I wanted a good dinner. We went out and we had a really nice time. I may not have remembered the name of the restaurant, but I remember laughing and enjoying his company.

The next day, I came into work and opened my computer to an email from him. He thanked me for a good time and said a few sweet things that made me smile. This happened every day for weeks. I would go to my desk and hurry to turn on my computer, excited for his message, because he made me laugh. It was an amazing way to start my day. I never had been with anyone that made me laugh like that. Because he did, I wanted to continue to get to know him. It felt so nice to be pursued and courted by a gentleman.

Dating him was a bit of a challenge though because sometimes, those morning emails were all I had. There was an adjustment period because he had always been very motivated about his work. This was not great by my definition because I needed someone to give me attention. This is normally where my pattern of looking outside of the relationship would kick in, but I was determined for it to go differently. This is also where my drinking normally escalated, but I was somehow able to resist.

When I started dating Ray, I was still drinking daily but I put up such a functional front that even I believed in. I tricked myself into thinking that if I looked good on the outside, excelled in my job, then everything truly was all good.

Because Ray and I approached relationship troubles differently, we didn't have a smooth start. He came from a home of stability and love, quite different from mine. There was no arguing in his home, and everything ended in an argument at mine. We were both operating from what we knew, but we also had very different value systems, completely different baselines. I had a long history of being unable to communicate in a healthy way.

I was focused on getting attention and Ray was focused on work. I tried hard to understand how much he valued work, but I was always determined to be number one on his list. Ranking second to work reignited some of those long-standing beliefs I grew up with, which fueled my drinking. His commitment to work first made me look at where my own values were, and navigating our relationship together became a consistent struggle. He also reevaluated his work/life balance, and after some time, we both committed to keeping each other a top priority, especially when we paved the way for family.

We had our ups and downs as any relationship does, but I knew he was different from the start. I knew from the person he was and the morals he had that his only intention was to marry me because he loved me. I knew that he courted me because he had decided after his investigation that I was someone I truly wanted to be with. Even though I understood all of that intellectually, I just wanted to feel like his number one. He may have loved me deeply, but I did not recognize it as the kind of love that I wanted.

Because I didn't love myself, I was always looking for others to fill that void for me. Ray was no exception. We had a lot of troubles in our first year of marriage. I struggled with jealousy over a woman I assumed he had feelings for, and this caused a lot of strife in our marriage. My unhealed past sometimes came close to sabotaging what I knew was a special relationship.

Of course, I blamed this all on my husband back then because I was always the victim, but thankfully since taking on my own healing and understanding as my responsibility, I see it differently. It took years to work out my past in a way that didn't affect my present. Spoiler alert, we are still together, but seeing us smiling and in love today is no indication of all that we went through to get where we are.

We met in 1998, got engaged in 2001, married in 2002, and had our son, Matthew, in 2003. The years went by fast and furiously. We were always working on getting along and I was often projecting my unhealed wounds onto him and the relationship. We were living in Manhattan Beach, California during those first years. I had a new baby, a dog named Biscuit, and a husband that loved me. On paper, it all checked out. Life should have been considered great and from the outside looking in, it was.

I was generally happy, but I still felt an emptiness because I was not getting what I thought I should be getting from my husband: the attention I so deeply craved. There was no substitute for this during those times. He worked, and I wanted him around more. I felt empty inside and miserably lonely.

Retiring from work to stay home with my son compounded my sorrow. I thought I was so excited for this opportunity, but it turned out to be nothing like I planned. I left work about three months before giving birth to get the house set up and it was lonely. This was uncharted territory for me, having never been alone much less lonely. I missed the commotion of the office and the attention I was able to get at my job. Work was what validated me. All I had known was work and I willingly gave that up. I struggled with that, and it became an undercurrent of the next phase of my life.

Once I had our son, there was great turmoil going on within me. I was still missing Ray while he was working. I was a new mom, a role that no one is ever truly prepared for. I no longer had a career identity, and I still harbored the rage and pain of my childhood creating a perfect storm for my alcoholism. I drank every day.

Ray and I went out socially on the weekends, and my husband gave me a hard time about what and how much I drank. I thought I was just having fun and being social. The people around me were drinking, too, but he was *not* having fun. I started to think *he* was just not fun. I kept drinking just to wash away the feeling of judgment and ignore his remarks.

Also, to get beyond of the judgment, I got involved in mom groups and found the moms that enjoyed an afternoon glass of wine. We had playdates for our kids so we could get together. I felt like I was in heaven living in Manhattan Beach with other women like me. The perfect bubble. I was making friends in a new life with my son, I was finding pockets of happiness with other moms who drank while their spouses were away at work.

Just as I was getting settled into this life, Ray was offered a new job opportunity in New York City. When our son was about two years old, we made the decision to move to Wyckoff, New Jersey, back to his roots. Sure, I was a bit bummed to leave the life I had set up, but I always loved a new beginning. This fit my pattern of starting over so I had the butterflies of excitement about a clean slate.

I was also very excited that we would have his family close so he and I could start over. I was ready for another chance at us. We found a house there and the move took us about three months. We lived apart during that time, so I was very excited once I was able to move to New Jersey. During those three months, I fantasized about our fresh start. I imagined Ray and I were going to have time to bond, enjoy New York City, and have his family help with our son. It seemed exciting and promising.

17

From Lonely to Lonelier

Once I got there, we settled into the new house pretty well. It was nice when Ray took me to the shore and showed me some of the places that he used to visit when he lived there growing up. I know it was nostalgic for him and it was nice to see. I absolutely loved the house he had picked for us, but all of a sudden, I was very lonely again because I didn't know anyone. I was discouraged about the idea of starting over this time because it felt more like a burden.

I didn't feel like I could catch a groove for quite some time because I didn't understand the area. A big factor of living where we did was the seasons. We moved to Wyckoff, New Jersey in April and everyone went away in June. Seasonal relocation was very new to me and anyone I had met when I got there left just after I got to know them.

We lived in a neighborhood, where people only visited for part of the year, and it was quite removed from shops and restaurants. I was used to walkable Manhattan Beach, where it was warm and sunny year-round, everyone was out and about, and there was always something to do or someone to see. I was trying to adjust, but this drove up my loneliness and my resentment for Ray's work schedule.

One glimmer of hope at the end of summer was the beginning

of the school year. I was glad that school was starting so I could start meeting other parents and so our son could get involved and make some friends as well. Things went well in school very quickly. I got involved and felt like I could make it work.

Soon after we arrived in our new home, I found out I was pregnant with our daughter, Grace. She truly has turned out to be the grace of God in my life, but I was disappointed to get pregnant so soon after arriving because I didn't get to enjoy New York City with Ray like I had hoped and planned. Once I got past my plans changing, I was able to focus on bringing baby number two into this world. During my pregnancies I was able to limit my drinking during this very important time of growing our babies, but I still had the occasional sip on a glass of wine, and in the third trimester, I enjoyed a glass on occasion.

When I was getting settled into our new environment, I was able to shift my focus to Matthew's schooling, Mommy and Me classes, and preparing for our daughter's arrival. Our son was about two and a half when she was born and thankfully, I had a nanny to help me. After giving birth, I was able to keep my drinking tamed. Just like any new relationship and every fresh start, it took a little while for my addiction to escalate.

Things were going well for a while. I think I was mostly distracted by having two children to look after so time flew by. I was still drinking, but this is one of those examples of thinking I was being discrete. I assumed that because I was involved with the kids and their schooling, no one could tell I was unhappy or drinking. I was balancing everything well and I even tried to start a business. I thought I had it all together, but I knew that I was mostly trying to distract myself.

I think it is important to say that I was drinking pretty much every day of my life. It never had to be much, but alcohol was certainly a part of my daily schedule. I bring this up because I can tell these stories of career and relationship transitions, and I know that a buzz or a hangover is a part of all the memories. At this phase of the facade, I thought I had everyone else fooled. I always chewed gum or brushed my teeth before getting somewhere and I was sure I had it under wraps.

It wasn't until my sobriety journey that I found out more people knew when I had been drinking than I realized. I always got my work done, but it wasn't always with a clear head.

Things started getting worse in our marriage. My husband was working a lot, and something was missing for me. I was very resentful of him. I was deeply lonely and that is not good for a person who lives with a black hole inside them and who also fills that void with alcohol and attention. My drinking started to escalate again to deal with my resentment and frustration.

In the thick of it, our relationship had gotten to the point where my husband and I did not like one another at all. We were fighting all the time. We both felt like we hated one another; we could barely look at each other. There were plenty of times I didn't think our marriage would survive. I never believed I could truly be loved, and I didn't have any reference for how to have a healthy relationship. This made working out our issues quite challenging.

At a low point, we finally decided to go to marriage counseling, and it went well. It was very helpful for me to have a professional explain to my husband why I was the way I was and why I needed what I needed. I didn't have the communication skills to help my husband understand the needs of someone who has been sexually abused and raised by an alcoholic mother. Of course, I felt it, but I had no idea how to explain it.

I couldn't put my feelings of abandonment into words and describe it the way our counselor did. I felt seen and heard in a whole new way. He was able to help me see for myself that whenever a man would tell me what to do, I felt like he was trying to be a father figure and control me. This caused me to resist my husband's requests to get healthy and stop drinking. He was open to listening, which I appreciated, but our progress was short-lived.

My husband worked so much he couldn't give me what I needed, and I wasn't very willing to slow down drinking. He was very responsive to what he learned about me in counseling, but I still didn't feel like I could be myself with him. I was still doing what I knew to do to cope with my pain and suffering so the drinking continued to escalate.

I remember right around that time being out drinking with some friends and I yelled out, "I can only be myself when I have some drinks and am with friends and *not* with my husband."

I cringe at that memory now. I *couldn't* have been myself back then. I didn't know who that person was. What I was doing was escaping. I was being a hurt little girl who didn't know how to get her real needs met. It was a messy time in my life.

Things only seemed to get messier because I had decided that what was missing in my life was my career. I knew that I wanted to do something that brought me back into the field of television, but this time, I decided that I wanted to get *in front* of the camera. I had spent my whole life behind the scenes in television and wanted to take my chances as a print model and commercial actress. I craved attention, and this was one way to get it!

At this point, I wanted out of my house and marriage so much that I was willing to go above and beyond to make my new career happen. I was sure this would fix everything in my life. Greater decline happened after I started acting. I was part of my son's school organizations and felt connected to people but at the same time it was hard to be part of any group. I got aggravated and was not the best team player because I was sensitive and would take everything personally. During these years I drank the most.

18

My Last Drink

I had my last drink on October 3, 2015. I had a modeling gig that day.

Struggling with my age, looks, loneliness, motherhood, and marriage, I decided to launch a new career as a model. I was looking for a way to feel revitalized. It dawned on me that it was finally time to pursue a lifelong dream. I had wanted to be a model since I was sixteen and decided to go for it.

The problem was that I was petrified to audition. It was important to have acting talent and be able to show it in a short window of opportunity to get gigs. I would have to play a role or make certain facial expressions on demand, and I was so nervous the entire time. I would shake, even for a picture being taken. I even went to acting school to learn but I was still so vulnerable to any feedback or criticism.

A woman like me, a survivor of sexual abuse, physical abuse, mental abuse, a daughter of an alcoholic mom, an absent alcoholic dad, and in a position to be judged over and over was a nightmare, yet crazy exciting. I didn't understand what would make me happy because my unhappiness crept even higher after I got in front of the camera. That is when the liquid courage came into play, and with week after week of the same thing, the drinking matched the level of my unhappiness.

Add the stress of the industry to my unhappiness and alcoholism, and it was a cocktail for disaster. I went to New York City for training, auditions, and jobs. I was at the mercy of the multiple agents I had, calling on me to be available for the client when they needed me. I didn't feel supported and became very resentful of my husband not being at home to help. I felt like I could not put my all into this new dream.

People offered the idea of getting a babysitter, but I had every excuse not to. I argued that my modeling schedule was too unpredictable, but I knew I wanted to raise my children myself. As a result of my own upbringing, I overcompensated with them. All I wanted to do was smother them with love. I somehow wanted my new career *and* my children, but I hadn't found a way to balance that yet. My kids were still young, and I wanted to be a part of their lives. I never wanted them to experience the kind of abuse or abandonment that I did.

Finding the balance in all of this was also an uphill battle with my husband. He wanted me home with the kids as much as I wanted to be there. He didn't discourage me or talk me out of following my career dreams, but I knew he preferred me to be present in our children's lives. He also knew how unhealthy my drinking was and wanted me to make taking care of myself a priority. He had an amazing job that provided us with a wonderful life. It wasn't that I needed to work for financial gains. Having a career was something I needed for my own validation. Being in front of the camera was a dream that I always had and felt ready to pursue. I wasn't doing it for the money—it was to fulfill the dream and to escape my reality.

As usual, I left the house with my thermos of wine, my liquid courage. I did this to take the edge off. I would sip it on the way and be feeling good by the time I arrived. That day, it was a runway show at Bloomingdale's. I arrived at Shorthills Mall and was trying to find the right department. I was getting nervous like I usually did before a show. I always felt a bit frantic, and my throat would get tight. The inner critic in my head yelled loudly on show days, and I was easily distracted by my thoughts.

I was headed up the escalator thinking about the wine in my thermos, telling myself I did not need it. I was telling myself that I could do it on my own, until I was told that I was in the wrong mall. The show was at Riverside Mall, thirty minutes away. I panicked.

I already showed up at Bloomingdale's behind schedule and suddenly, I was told I had to get somewhere else. I hustled out, trying not to completely freak out, but I was so upset. I got in my car and drove as fast as I could to make it before the show. Trying to calm down, I drank the entire thermos of wine on the way. I was so stressed and for me, wine was the answer. I got to the mall just in time to find the department and get my clothes. I was feeling good by the time I walked. I could hardly believe I made it, but I did. When the stressful part was over, I was in a better mood.

A friend of mine came to see the show, and we went to lunch at the mall after the show. I was so ready to unwind after such a stressful few hours! My kids were at home with a babysitter, and this was a free day out for me. I loved the opportunity to get out of the house for the day, so I felt like taking advantage of some girl time.

I started off with a personal favorite, a dirty martini, and ordered fish. I ate very little because I was always trying to stay thin. When it came to the choice between alcohol or food, I went for the alcohol. After the martini, I had a glass of wine.

I was going to go home but my friend asked about stopping off for another drink. At this point, I was in no frame of mind to make a good decision, so I went. I had another glass of wine, and I knew I needed to eat. My friend wanted another drink, so I joined. I ordered the next glass of wine, and I don't remember what I did next.

What I do know is that I got in my car and left. My friend went to the ladies' room, and I made the decision to leave. Still, I do not know how I nearly got home. I was not coherent until I was standing outside of my car, failing a sobriety test, and being arrested.

I sobered up a bit on my ride to the station thinking of how I was going to hide this from my husband. There was no way I was going to let my husband know what had happened. There had to be a way to hide this from him. I was trying to think straight but I was spinning, mainly from the wine but also fear. *How am I going to pull this off?* I wondered.

When I was given my phone call, I called my friend Sally, a drinking buddy, to come pick me up once I was released. I knew she'd help me figure this out. Sally rushed into the station, with her oversized purse slapping against her thin hip, but I lost my breath when I saw my husband walk in with her. They happened to show up at the same time. I thought I was going to faint.

I couldn't believe my eyes. I was panicking and trying to figure out how Ray knew I had gotten arrested. I wanted to disappear. I wanted to run away, and I even considered leaving with Sally and just never looking back. I was ashamed to my core. I could hardly stand the ache of shame I felt. The pang of that level of embarrassment was unbearable but I didn't run. I let my husband bail me out, and I left that police station in total defeat and rage.

I later found out that the police had called my husband. The look of disdain on his face said it all for me. He was as tired of my drinking as I was of him. He was cordial with the police, thanked them for all they had done, and we headed home, but home with him was the last place I wanted to go. You might think I'd be apologizing for this mess I made but I had so much anger toward him and our marriage. It was his fault, after all. I really did want to run away.

And I almost lost that life, the very life I tried to escape.

Getting to this rock bottom had been a few years in the making. You don't just wake up an alcoholic one day. It is days, months, and years of wondering, thinking, knowing—deep down— something is wrong. I knew for some time that I should slow down or quit but at that point, I had no control. I thought I wanted out of the life I had, my marriage, perhaps a fresh start would fix things, and drinking was my escape. We had kids and houses and cars and bills. We were so connected that I had no idea how to leave other than drink and follow my dreams of modeling. The way I always left situations, relationships, and circumstances was so easy before. I know now that

I was trying to fill something. I was trying to feel anything other than the hate, anger, and rage I had in my heart.

I was so lonely. My husband worked all the time and I had given myself completely to my family. I was raising kids and had lost myself in that role. Was I *just* a wife to an absent man? Was I *just* Matthew's and Grace's mom? This life was something I believed I wanted for myself, but it was consuming me. The only love I felt was for my children, and even that was not enough. I was struggling with motherhood and loneliness. I was spiraling in self-hatred, sadness, and abandonment.

Something else I was struggling with was aging as I believed that all I had to offer was what was on the outside. It always worked in the past, and it helped keep me distracted from what was going on inside me.

Looking good was what I focused on and perfected; it was what I believed I could control. After children and with the years flying by, a wrinkle here or a gray hair there started to freak me out. Aging made my self-worth even lower, and it had never been very high.

My dream of modeling quickly turned into a nightmare when my low self-esteem and anxiety surfaced in front of the camera. The dream I assumed would lift me up threw me deeper into pain, anger, fear, and drinking. I cringed at the thought of all the judgment and criticism of the modeling and acting industry. I never felt good enough or pretty enough and in turn, was always criticizing myself. I don't know why I thought I could ever actually be successful.

All this thinking crashed down on me. I was living this nightmare in the passenger seat on our way back home from the police station. We drove the whole way home without speaking. We pulled into the garage, still not a word spoken. The tension between us was painful and palpable. He was gripping the steering wheel tightly and I could feel the heat of my rage burning in every cell of my body. I wanted to explode. I wanted to scream. I wanted him to lecture me so I could blow off some steam. I longed for escape. I felt caged and trapped, with no way out. I hated myself as much as I thought I hated him.

Our beautiful home in Wyckoff, New Jersey was on one of the

most sought-after streets in the town, with a golf course that backed up to our yard. It was a prestigious neighborhood, and I sank into my seat and ducked my head as we turned onto our block, shame holding me down. When we pulled in, I jumped out of the car, rushed into the house, and apologized to the babysitter for getting home so late. I was hoping she had no idea about how my day went. I didn't want to get close enough for her to smell the alcohol on my breath. I was still intoxicated at this point and trying to act straight and sober. I don't know how well that went over but it didn't matter. I am sure she knew something was up. I never stayed out late like that, especially without being in communication.

I was so distraught that I could hardly form sentences. I said goodnight to my children and excused myself. It was seven in the evening, but this day had felt like four days in one. I couldn't stay up for another minute. My husband said we would speak in the morning, so I stumbled up to the guest room in utter shame and passed out.

Leading up to this moment, I had never hit anything that I would call rock bottom, but when I woke up the next morning, I knew that is exactly what had happened. I woke up with a wicked hangover and the ache of true sorrow and regret for what I had done. I have no idea how I didn't harm myself or anyone else. I am so endlessly grateful for that fortune, but it didn't alleviate the pain of how stupid I had been. I could hardly believe I had gotten to this point. I lay there thinking about the events of the day before and all the days leading up to that point. I allowed myself to see what was happening—or maybe I was forced. Either way, I was in the middle of something big.

All of 2014, my husband had been asking and urging me to get healthy, but what I heard him say was to quit drinking. *He can't control me, and besides, I'm in therapy. My therapist hasn't told me to stop. I'm fine.* I was still trying to pursue acting and modeling, which had increased my drinking. My resentment of him could no longer be contained. I just wanted out.

In fact, I specifically remember going to a Halloween party in 2014 and Ray was urging me to stop drinking. Some nights leading up to this, he'd asked how many I'd had, or maybe he just said something like haven't you had enough, either way, his judgment of me was making me crazy! At this point, I specifically said to him that I *wasn't* an alcoholic. I swore I could control my drinking, so I only had one glass of wine that night to prove my point.

This was also the time in my life where I was starting to secretly ask *myself* if I had a problem. I had no idea about the progression of alcoholism or alcohol use disorder. For years and years, I had a vicious cycle of waking up in the middle of the night and telling myself that I was not going to drink the next day. I would wake up and Google different ways to finally quit. I would promise myself that I was finally done. I would read over Dr. Google's suggestions night after night.

There was a part of me that knew I didn't want to quit, so I was mostly looking for solutions that would help me manage my consumption. I believed I still had some control. I was trying to find ways that weren't sobriety or recovery. There were always suggestions like hypnosis, acupuncture, staying busy with different hobbies, volunteer work, and more. There were endless articles of what could help, but nothing did—nothing I actually tried anyway. I knew deep in my heart that I needed to go to a recovery program and go through the recommended steps completely. I often landed on an article about recovery, mostly of the 12-Step programs available, but I would never go back. I didn't want to be sober; I just didn't want to struggle the way that I had been. All I would ever do was read about it and then go back to bed.

This was a recurring pattern for years, but especially in 2014, the year before my arrest. Waking up feeling guilty and terrible, promising, researching, dozing back off, waking up, and never following through. I always went back. I always drank again the next day.

Failing at quitting every day was maddening. It continuously pushed me deeper into depression and drinking was the solution to the way it all felt. I spiraled day in and day out. My body was under so much distress from this cycle, and I felt hopeless on the deepest level. This was the first time, in October 2014, that I accepted that I needed to go to the 12-Step program, exactly one year before my rock bottom. I figured a few meetings would do me good. That early DUI in college and the forged signatures of a program didn't count. I decided to give it a try.

I broke down and went. My first meeting was an all-women's meeting in Ridgewood, New Jersey. It was definitely hard to walk into that room. I was at a low point. I did admit and introduce myself as an alcoholic and everyone was very inviting. I met some wonderful women that took me under their wing.

I only attended for about three months before I started sizing myself up to others in the room. Comparatively, I wasn't nearly as bad as the women in these meetings. They would tell their stories and I would say to myself, "I'm not that way. I'm not drinking all day. I'm not *that* bad. I don't do *that*. I have a good life. I'm good to my children. I just have a little too much wine."

My own facade fooled me. I convinced myself I was not like them, and I did not have a problem. I told myself that no one thought I was an alcoholic so I must not have been. I concluded that I was just overreacting. I also convinced myself that I could get it under control. I mean, I'd done it before. *Hadn't I?*

It took one more year for my life to completely disintegrate. I was not getting to do what I wanted so I lashed out by drinking more. I was sneaking wine so my husband wouldn't know and going out as much as I could with friends who drank like me. I'm the only one who knew, and I refused to admit it.

My husband started a new job and he wanted me to play the executive wife. He wanted me to be a different person and live a different life. I now understand the pressure that he was being put under at work, but at that time I became resentful of him. I remember the white-hot rage that I felt toward him for feeling like he was trying to control my life and change me.

I drank *at* him. I drank because he told me not to. I drank because I wanted to, and no one was going to tell me what to do. I wanted out of my marriage, but I feared he would take the children from me.

I drank to punish him for how trapped I felt.

I will never forget October 4th, 2015, as the day I admitted to myself and my husband that I was an alcoholic. There was no doubt and no denying it. No longer could I hide. No longer could I rationalize. I hit the wall where even I could not escape myself. I knew this was the end of the road for me and alcohol. I could not believe it had come to this, and yet, it was necessary. I clearly needed a major consequence to quit, and that day, I had it.

A lifetime of drowning my fear, anger, and pain had come to a head. It took me until forty-six to see the error in my ways, but I never had the love and support in my life like the love of my husband. He loved me dearly, but my alcoholism blinded me to what I had, and the cumulative pain of my past was an insurmountable challenge for him.

After decades of chaos and using alcohol, it was time to quit. It was time to get help. It was time to surrender to something greater than my addiction. I often share that the idea to never drink again is truly daunting. Quitting drinking was the hardest decision I have ever made in my life, but it was also the best one.

PART 3

From Victim to Survivor

19

Feeling True Love from a Man for the First Time

When I woke up the morning after my DUI, I spent a bit of time in the guest room admitting to myself that I was an alcoholic. It was an undeniable fact at his point. I knew I had to face it and I also knew that I had to face my husband. When I went downstairs, he was already awake and in the living room. He asked me to join him on the couch. I was so uncomfortable to face what I had done, but I knew that if I did nothing, I would lose everything.

I sat down and sunk into the couch. I was in tears. I was defeated and drained. I remember being angry the day before, but I didn't have any fight left in me. At that moment, I looked into my husband's eyes and the words came out, "I'm an alcoholic."

My husband reached out and embraced me. I was able to let go of all the tension in my body, and I let myself fall apart. I didn't have to lie anymore. I didn't have to pretend or numb or hide anymore. My addiction was out in the open. It is difficult to articulate the heart-wrenching pain of complete surrender, but my whole body went limp in his arms, and I let it. I sobbed in relief as he held me tightly.

As if something magical had happened, I felt the weight of the world drop from my shoulders for the first time. On a cellular level, I could feel myself transforming from the inside out.

Sitting on that couch, in my husband's embrace, was the first time I truly felt loved. It was at that moment that I realized he was the man I had hoped for my whole life. We had been married for years and I never truly recognized him as the man who would make it all better. He was right in front of me all this time, but finally, my heart and mind *saw* him. I felt a wave of peace come over me. A peace that had long been missing.

My husband looked me straight in the eyes and let me know that he would help in any way he could. I had never felt love like that, ever. It was the safest I had ever felt. I will never forget that moment for as long as I live. It was as if the decades of living as a victim and in pain were overcome by the love of that hug from my husband. I made the commitment to myself and him that I would get healthy and sober. My healing journey started that day.

20

From Victim to Survivor

Experiencing love like that for the very first time changed me eternally. I crossed a threshold in my life and I knew there was no going back. It was time to get sober.

It was that very same day I went an Alcoholics Anonymous meeting. My car had been impounded, so with our children in tow, Ray dropped me off at a meeting in Oakland, New Jersey. It was a Sunday. Although I knew I was ready, I was equally as apprehensive. I had already failed my previous attempt the year before so I had all sorts of assumptions running in my head about how it could potentially go.

I was riddled with guilt and shame for getting behind the wheel of a car and putting myself and others in grave danger. I was beside myself thinking that I had gotten into my car to drive while blackout drunk. I had lost control over myself, my drinking, and my judgment. I was embarrassed, and even though I knew a 12-Step program was what I needed, I was cringing inside about what I had done.

I was terrified, so I reached out to the woman that I had met when I tried going a year earlier. Her name was Debbie. I shuffled out of the car, still hungover. Debbie met me outside and greeted me with a big smile and a hug. I was a wreck inside and trying to hold it together on the outside, but her hug made me feel safe. I held onto that feeling as we walked into that new first meeting.

I could hardly keep myself together and left for the bathroom when the room wouldn't stop spinning. It was partially the hangover and partially the realization that I landed myself in this position. Me. This was my fault. The whole weekend seemed more like a movie scene than my real life.

I ran to the bathroom to throw up and that helped me come down from my hangover and nerves. As I washed my face and hands, I took a good hard look at myself in the mirror. I wanted life to be better, but I was so scared of myself. I was terrified of what it meant to be sober. I feared actually facing myself and life without alcohol. I stared at that tired (and I mean soul-level tired) mother and wife and prayed to a God I didn't fully know. "Please make it stop, God. Please help me stop."

I wanted to be done but I knew I couldn't do it alone; I needed help. I knew I needed to head back into that meeting, and so I did.

I went through the ritual of introducing myself as an alcoholic and at this point in the day, I had already admitted it twice. I know it sounds funny, but I started to feel a difference, like I was already starting to take more responsibility for my life and my actions. Everyone was inviting, and I started to realize I was not alone in my feelings or strife. Believe me, up to this point, I thought I was the only one. I considered myself alone on this journey, with no one to understand me, and certainly no one to help me. I felt safe and welcomed and it was exactly what I needed at a time when I was experiencing so much shame.

I went that day, the first step in the right direction, and I never looked back. In retrospect, I know that it was this meeting and my hard work that saved my life. After the meeting, Debbie agreed to sponsor me. I was so grateful. While I felt love from my husband that morning, it's the embrace of my new sponsor helping me get started with the program that helped the transformation take off.

I felt comfortable with her support and guidance, so we went to work immediately. I agreed with her, and myself, to do everything asked of me. I felt like she was an angel sent directly to help me, because the shame I struggled with could have stopped my progress multiple times, but she was there for me every time I ran into a new roadblock. We were able to navigate the journey together.

One of my biggest roadblocks was my victimhood. I played that role well. I always blamed my struggles on others, which never helped the situation. I had endless reasons to feel like a victim and many of them were very valid, but it wasn't until doing the work that I got a full understanding of how I used my own story to disempower myself. I knew this wouldn't work for the rest of my life. I had to change.

I often told myself that I acted that way because no one understood what I had been through. I believed that no one could understand me because they hadn't gone through what I had. I used it to justify my drinking, my self-destructive behaviors, my ineffective and inappropriate coping strategies, and my lashing out. I often tried to validate and excuse myself for acting the way that I did because I had been through so much torment and again, I convinced myself that I had every reason to justify my behaviors. The problem was it wasn't getting me anywhere I was happy with or proud of.

One of the things I realize now was that because of my experiences as a young child and growing up in the unpredictable and unsafe environments is that I stored in the recesses of my mind absolutely everything that happened. On an energetic level, it set me up to vibrate at very low frequencies as I was riddled with shame, guilt, and fear. I have learned that my repeating of cycles was truly not my fault because it was the only way I knew. But that had to end once I was in adulthood. I had to take responsibility. When I was a child, each negative experience boxed me in and conditioned me to repeat my own reaction. I didn't have a healthy role model to show me how to release negativity to ensure it didn't dictate my reaction the next time.

I was sure that it was everyone else's fault that my life was the way it was. In fact, I shared my woes with anyone who would listen because I mostly felt like my parents were to blame for the way that

I had turned out. My abandonment issues fueled my victimhood for most of my life.

I felt banished, abandoned, and betrayed by both my mom and my dad. That feeling and fear shaped the way I saw everything. It distorted the way I saw the world, myself, relationships, and so much more. I was afraid of everyone else abandoning me throughout my life because of it. Every relationship felt risky. I feared that people were going to hurt me and/or leave me. I had no ability to form lasting relationships with people, so I was the one who had to abandon people. This felt better than being abandoned so I learned to use this strategy to my advantage. My fear of being abandoned ran my thoughts, actions, and decisions, and led to a ton of chaos.

Once my children were born, I decided that I never wanted them to feel abandonment. Throughout their lives, I was always there, doing everything for them. I overcompensated by trying to show them the love I never had. Ironically, toward the end of my drinking, it seemed obvious that I *was* abandoning them. I got so wrapped up in myself for a while that I started choosing drinking, working, and what I wanted instead of prioritizing family.

Thankfully, they were young, and they didn't really see what was happening. At the height of my anger and drinking, I wanted to leave everything I loved behind. I was on the brink of ruining everything I loved because I was breaking and drinking to try to keep it together. I almost lost the very life I tried to escape.

It was through working the steps, especially step four, that I came to understand I was creating my own chaos. The chaos caused by the combination of victimhood and alcoholism is disastrous. I was absolutely falling apart in every way. The decades' worth of unhealed pain had finally become too much to bear. I was trying to keep it all together and simultaneously wanting to run from it all. My solution to feeling stuck was to drink, but I was just destroying myself more and more.

Deep down, I knew these truths, but I had been drowning them with wine. I could not have any lasting realizations or breakthroughs while under the influence; I lived in a fog, a blur. It was my sobriety that led me to make lasting shifts in my consciousness. The conscious shift I had to make was from identifying as a victim to living as a survivor.

Whether you are trying to get sober or not, the rest of this book will offer you insights and opportunities to level up in the overall quality of your life.

You may be searching for a way out of addiction. Whether you are on day one of sobriety, day one hundred, or one thousand, I commend you. You may be supporting a family member or friend in making this change. Maybe you are reading for some other reason. While there are many experts out there to help, I simply want to share what got me through to the other side. Is my way the only way? Absolutely not, but I was able to improve the overall quality of my life with some practices that may also help you (or someone you love).

If you are not recovering from any specific substance, consider that we are also subtly addicted to coping mechanisms like drama, gossip, overwhelm, and distraction. We can be addicted to working, attention, achieving, and more. What about our pesky cell phones? Many don't believe it, but there is plenty of research out there now about how even a ding on a phone can give us a hit of dopamine that is impossible to ignore.

I had to sober up from my addiction to my victimhood and take responsibility for my life. I had to give up the idea that everything was happening *to* me and that everyone was out to get me. I got just as intoxicated on anger and blame which impaired my judgment as much as the wine. When I began my recovery, I began to shift my idea of who and what had control.

That control shifted away from the blame I held against my parents and husband and back onto me. I decided to take back my power and step up as the leader of my life. During the time in my involvement with this program, I worked the steps and chose to identify as a survivor.

I do have to tell you that this wasn't a shift that happened overnight. Just because you come to realize your victimhood doesn't mean you can immediately put an end to it. Just like with substance use disorder, it's a process. The journey of recovery goes something like this for many people: the first stage is what is called precontemplation where there's absolutely no recognition of drinking (or whatever you are using to cope) as a problem. In my case, it's obvious I stayed there for many years. Next is the contemplation stage, where there's the nagging question mark within, recognizing there *could* be an issue, yet denying it vehemently, or deciding that some changes probably should happen to prove to self that it's not really "that bad." Again, in my own journey with my husband wanting me to get healthier or in my rationalizing that the wine I carried around was just to soothe my nerves, the seed had been planted.

On some level, I believe I knew I had a problem, but was not ready for change. In the preparation stage, a person starts to plan for what changes they will make: Will they drink less, or stop altogether? Will they still hang out with drinking friends, or will they break off friendships? To what degree will they change their lives?

For me, that fateful day of the arrest changed my life *for* me. I thrust myself straight into the next stage: the action stage. This is where all the changes contemplated and planned must be executed. This stage is extremely stressful, and often ends in relapse. This is the phase where all the thinking and planning must be proven, revised, and perhaps replanned for success. For me, it was a matter of life and death where I committed myself to living. I'd forced my own hand and couldn't relapse. I chose to live. I chose to be a survivor. I chose to keep my family. The last of the five stages is maintenance. All the things that help get a person to the action stage must be maintained, monitored, and updated if needed to ward off complacency. Relapse also often happens here because many believe they have beaten alcoholism and can have "just one glass" and be okay.

The entire recovery path is the healing process. At every stage, and at every challenge there is a chance to acknowledge shortcomings and heal. When I shifted my mindset and my identity from victim to survivor, I had to heal the wounds that fueled my fire for playing the victim. I knew it was time to take responsibility for how the rest of my life was going to go. While I did not have a choice in what happened to me at six or even twelve, it was absolutely my choice what would happen from this day forward.

I am filled with gratitude for my journey—the good, the bad, and the embarrassing. My past does not define me. My trauma does not limit me. I am a survivor. I feel like I'm born again. I have a new chance at life, and I am going to live it in grace and gratitude.

21

The Healing Process

The healing process looks different for people, and while I cannot speak to how others have gotten to the other side, I can certainly speak to how I have arrived where I am. There are proven recovery methods, styles, and schools of thought. I found my initial healing during that first day in the 12-Step meeting; I knew I was in the right place. As hard as it was to be there, both physically and emotionally, it felt right. My sponsor helped me every step of the way, and if you are just starting this part of the journey, or supporting someone else who is on it, just know that sponsors come in all shapes, colors, genders, etc. Find someone who you know deep within will help you get to where you want to be, because there may be a time where they literally save your life by being there for you. If you don't go the AA route, find one that you can commit to.

I began that day to bond with others, learn tools, read *The Big Book*, give of myself, and give myself time in the program. I was very willing to make the changes that the program offered, but it didn't make it any less challenging during the process. On top of my sponsor's accountability, I had to incorporate new practices that would keep me showing up for the work. It was a daily commitment and a full-time job.

Healing takes a lot out of you! One of the most effective strategies I used was napping often. I remember how deeply tired I was when I stopped drinking. Once the fog of consistent drinking lifted, the real layers of shame and guilt were there to deal with and recover from. My mind, body, heart, and soul were tired of the facade I had been holding up all those years, decades even. I had layers and layers to peel back. Sometimes they fell away, and other times, the struggle was real!

I remember feeling my body start to relax over time and when I let go of the performance of trying to be perfect or keeping it all together, I practically felt like I was melting. Instead of crumbling like when I was drinking, I felt like I was falling apart in a constructive way—falling apart to eventually come back together.

I went to bed exhausted on many occasions because I could hardly take another step forward. I withheld my own judgment and let this happen because deeper than my exhaustion was the knowledge that my body was restoring itself. I needed that rest and I finally let myself have it. I especially felt justified in my rest because I was showing up for the hard work of my sobriety journey.

While I have no doubt that everyone's heard of the efficacy of Alcoholics Anonymous 12-Step program, I just want to point a few things you may not know if you have never been on the journey. Yes, there are twelve steps, and while attendees are urged to work them in order, some of the steps take many months, even years, to work through. And once you work the step, it doesn't mean you never go back and rework it. Thank goodness there's a book called *The Big Book of Alcoholics Anonymous* that helps guide a person along. The book has a plain cover, so unless people around know, they wouldn't know what you are reading. This is helpful to many as recovery is often very personal. Many people become "lifers" where they show up to meetings as diligently on day 5,791 as they did on day thirty or even day one. That is not necessary, required, or even recommended for everyone. For some, being a lifer will be the way to continue to give back, to serve. For others, personal direction blended with spiritual calling could take them away from AA on their commitment to sobriety. There is no single right way to recover from any addiction or to commit to a life of joy. Just find a place to begin and do the work.

Regardless of the method or program one decides on for recovery, the absolute first step is admission. That step is repeated often as that's the way meetings open: introductions followed by "...and I'm an alcoholic." Remember all the years I said I wasn't? Remember how I always compared myself to those around me, or those who I believed were the "real" alcoholics? This step is ego-crushing on so many levels, and the utterance of those four words have the power to initiate great change, even if it takes years to jump into action.

Because I'd found a program with people that I liked, I was speaking openly and honestly, asking for help, trusting the process, and working the steps. I did as much of my own work as I could until I couldn't go forward alone and then I would surrender to rest. But my work was not limited to my meetings or the program. I also read and researched, dug into different schools of thought about addiction and recovery, and explored various modalities to health and joy. Rest was instrumental every step of the way. During that rest, my subconscious was doing work to connect me back with my higher self, a part of me that knew my own divinity. This wasn't a comfortable process, and I had days of fear and doubt. I spent many of those days in a chapel praying and committing myself to God and the new path I was paving for my life. You see, the second step is to admit that a power greater than oneself can restore the sanity that has been absent throughout the struggle with alcohol (or other substances, behaviors, or habits). That power for me is God first, then more personally, Jesus. There are plenty who use different words to name their power, and that is for them to tell.

Most days after a meeting I went into the beautiful little attached chapel. The meeting was held in the common room at the church (many recovery programs meet at religious places, but many do not; again, choose what works for you). Most people left quickly or stayed in the common room to socialize but I was drawn to the chapel.

Some days, I had fellow attendees in there with me, but most days, I had the sacred space to myself. I still get butterflies in my stomach remembering the soft, quiet, still energy in the chapel. I think the stillness provided a feeling of safety I couldn't get anywhere else.

There was a red carpet and two steps to kneel on leading up to the pulpit and altar. It was always decorated for the season, but I only went after meetings and never saw it filled during a church service. It was a private sanctuary for me.

As I exited the church, there was a large stained glass window depicting Jesus with sheep all around his feet and a lamb in his arms. Something else that stood out was a small picture of a lamb, painted in gold near the altar. I prayed to that gold lamb and Jesus in the stained glass asking him, nearly begging him, to help me through my road to sobriety. I prayed to that image of Jesus and said I wanted to be that lamb in his arms. I spoke to him in faith that I was heard and admitted that I wanted to be like those sheep following him, that he was my shepherd. I promised him many times that if I got through this phase of my life, I would always follow him. I asked him to change me into a person who could live without alcohol. I promised to never leave him if he would please help me through, and he did. He listened and he answered. I felt him take away my desire for alcohol.

While this is an incredible way to live life, the work is required. It wasn't a magical, simple transformation. It was one thing to put the drink down—that was just drowning out the pain and memory. It was another thing to give my life over to the saving grace of Jesus Christ—that was the strength that pulled me through the mess. It was up to me to follow through on the necessary healing. Words and prayer alone would never work. That's where the biggest changes started to happen.

I had to change my mindset and reprogram my brain. The way I'd been living was simply no longer working! I had to resolve parts of my past that I had never faced and had previously been unwilling to unpack. I had been in therapy for many years, but the process of this program and taking responsibility is how I managed. Perhaps the sessions and therapy before this moment helped prepare me for these much deeper shifts; perhaps not.

The twelve steps provide powerful guidance whether someone struggles with addiction or not. It was in the action of participating in those steps with support where the healing happened. I gained freedom, authenticity, and choice when I started to heal because I no longer told my story for attention. I was beginning to drop my past as my identity and therefore, alcohol was no longer my constant companion.

In the next chapter, I am going to share my walk through the twelve steps, but here, I want to share some of the day-to-day tools that were truly remarkable in the start of my healing. These are small steps you can take toward living your fullest life without overwhelming yourself and stopping before you start. These little tools helped me feel victorious even when my journey felt daunting.

The first, and my favorite, tool is the Serenity Prayer:

God, grant me the serenity to accept the things I cannot change, the courage to change the things I can, and the wisdom to know the difference.

This prayer saved me. I say it in my sleep these days. This is a prayer everyone in the AA program is served to memorize and use frequently. As a survivor, one of the things I had to come to terms with is that there are things out of my control. I had to accept things that didn't make sense and apologies that I never received. There are many aspects of my life and past that an older version of myself didn't have the capacity and wherewithal to understand. For that version of me, I pray this prayer. It helps me forgive, bless, and release what feels bigger than me or my understanding.

The next cue is: *Move a muscle, change a thought.*

I have a vivid memory of this reminder working for me one evening. It was early in my sobriety journey and Ray was away for work. I was watching TV and I got the urge to have some wine. No one was around. He wouldn't have known, and I am sure I could have gotten away with it. It was while I was contemplating the wine that I remembered this tool. "Move a muscle, change a thought," popped into my mind like a light-bulb kind of idea. So, instead of grabbing a bottle of wine, I got up, grabbed my Big Book, and started reading. In no time, I was back on track with my thoughts of clarity and commitment.

Next up: *Give of yourself and get out of yourself.*

Giving of yourself allows you to get out of your own head and it allows you to connect with others. Getting out of your own head is just about one of the best things an addict can do. Our addiction lives primarily in our thoughts. Granted, we know our bodies are storehouses for memories, triggers, blockages, and more, but it is our thinking brain that tends to obsess and strategize our demise. To give of ourselves and our time can bring us into our reality and out of our head. This is a great strategy for someone having a hard time going at it alone. When you commit to service, you are almost always interacting with others. Remember, connection is key.

Speaking of connection, the next tool: *Call someone in the program.*

Ask for help. This can be a huge challenge for many of us. Believe it or not, others truly want to help; they want to share the magic of what they have learned with you. Remember my last tip, give of yourself, and get out of yourself? That's exactly what others in the program are doing when they make themselves available for you. It's what being a sponsor is all about.

Getting a sponsor to walk the journey with is very helpful for guidance through the program in a way that causes a lasting shift. Per the program recommendation, ninety meetings in ninety days with a sponsor can really cause a turn-around that most addicts cannot create on their own. It is amazing how much change happens in ninety days. It's incredible because by this stage you start to feel the happiness promised in the program. They call that happiness *the pink cloud.*

Next tip: *The gratitude jar.*

This is a practice of finding something you're grateful for each day. I love this one. I had a couple of gratitude jars and a box. (They also make great gifts.) I said something I was grateful for each day out loud. I then wrote it down and put it in the jar. The motivating and rewarding part was reading them at the end of the year. It was always such a special and refreshing treat to remember my year that way. Even the toughest years had amazing memories and highlights. This taught me the powerful tool of reframing my memories.

22

My Journey Through the 12-Step Program

My healing process, my walk with the Divine, and my journey through the recovery are practically synonymous. They all happened at the same time and were interwoven in the way they moved me forward. I am not sure I would have stayed sober if it weren't for the 12-Step program. I am not sure I would have felt supported enough to heal if it weren't for the relationships I established with the spiritual world, Debbie, and the program. I am sure that my healing fueled my faith and sobriety.

For reference, there are *many* support structures like the 12-Step program I attended. If you research your addiction, it is likely there is a (free) support group for you. I mention free because I am aware that there are millions of people who don't get the help they so desperately need because they don't have the finances, insurance, or resources to access effective support. Do not let money be the reason you don't get help. Support is just on the other side of admitting, "I need help." My time in this program legitimately saved my life, and yet there was a time I felt I no longer identified with the four words that were so pivotal for me to admit initially: *and I'm an alcoholic.* I did so much self-healing and inner work over the years, that I actually changed the narrative. I changed MY narrative from victim to survivor. I outgrew the label *alcoholic* with daily practice, new routines and rituals, support, and faith.

There are also very valuable outlets like therapy, counseling, coaching, group programs, and more. There are books, podcasts, documentaries, and movies that will educate and inspire, motivate and sustain you when times get tough. There are professional services which may have a financial investment to them but if you have the resources, they can be very effective and supportive as well. Oftentimes, this includes more one-on-one work and that may serve you in a new way to take your inner work to the next level. Many, like me, find that beneath their addictions lie unhealed trauma from the past. Sorting through childhood confusion often requires a therapist or counselor. If those are not available for whatever reason, just start somewhere. Some free self-help work you can do is meditation, exercise, journaling, and reading, and there are many other support strategies and groups too, like finding a spiritual director, a club or meetup group and more.

Just in case the message isn't crystal clear here, I am inviting you to get help, support, and guidance in any way you have access, in whatever way resonates with you. I could *not* have turned my life around on my own. Many can. The burden was too heavy to bear alone. I did not have the mental, emotional, or spiritual tools to make the changes that saved my life. I was doing the best I could to survive my pain, but the tool I relied upon the most was alcohol.

I now fully understand how I used this tool of destruction. It was a coping mechanism used to try to feel better momentarily. I tried working my way to feeling better by achieving success, titles, validation, recognition, and accolades. I tried dating, and dating more, and dating again to find that perfect guy that would make me feel whole. I tried looking good to attempt to feel good and that never worked either. I used what I knew, but those couldn't heal my broken heart. I looked outside of myself in all ways before recognizing that the only path to feel better, was to get past—to get beyond—unhealthy lifestyle choices. Those attempts at coping couldn't resolve the pain of my wounded, traumatized inner child. I needed help, and so, I asked for and accepted it.

Allowing and inviting help are huge. Again, I say this from my own perspective, and I have seen many of these traits shared in doing the healing with and around others. As victims of abuse growing up in dysfunctional homes, we often conclude that we are undeserving of love. Especially outside of our family, when love and help is just offered without conditions or expectations, we can become suspicious of what the cost or penalty might be. No matter how desperately we may need or want help, our trauma response can often be to watch out for a potential threat of someone's kindness and generosity. This strategy may have helped us in the past, but it's time to put that down and face things head-on.

I had only myself to lean on for so long. I put up barriers to cope. I pushed the support of others away for years because I couldn't see my part in it all. I was also suspicious of anyone offering something as I felt there might be a hidden agenda or I'd have to endure some icky action in return. It seriously felt impossible to ask for help. I didn't feel like anyone understood what I had been through and the trauma I had held onto.

I didn't listen to the feedback of the people who cared about me because I had lost a lot of hope and trust and believed that most people were out to take advantage of me. I felt like I was on my own in many ways, and for a long time, I struggled silently and alone, even in my marriage. I did this until I literally couldn't. I know I am not the only one.

I began to understand all of this once I embraced sobriety. I never had people stand up for me the way Ray and my sponsor did, and it helped me get my footing to walk this path boldly.

I also prayed every day for clarity and to help me stay on track. My prayers and faith guided me to new heights in life. As humans, we are challenged to follow through and stay true to our commitments. This was made possible by my own spirituality and the structure of the program.

To recap: The first step is to admit powerlessness over alcohol and that life is unmanageable. The second step is to embrace that a power greater than ourselves can restore us to sanity. This is a simple admission that we have tried things our way for so long, and it has not gotten us any peace; in fact, it's brought us to our own version of rock bottom, of hopelessness. To make a change, here's where people must admit, invite, and accept that there are powers much greater than us that can help. Many fall back on their childhood religion, and if that works, great. Many have had religious or church-family traumas and returning to the source of trauma would never work. It's why this step is wide open for interpretation. Truly, this can be *any* power greater than ourselves.

The third step invites us to turn our will and our lives over to the care of God as we understand him (or her or it).

I did not struggle much with the idea of God taking over my life. I sure wasn't doing a great job, so I was willing to let someone else steer for a while, but I still had to learn how to allow that power to be in control. I was always trying to control my life and outcomes. Surrender became the real challenge and lesson. Through this work, I connected to my understanding of God in a very different way. With prayer, meditation, and a different world view, I was able to turn my life over and have the Divine fully guide me into a life of happiness. As a result, I felt more joy than ever before.

There are many ways to interpret "God" and while the traditional Christian teachings work for some, this step can be a turn-off for many. It's no reason to leave a program. One can be atheist or agnostic and still work through this step. It's a matter of looking around and recognizing what the "greater power" is for them. Maybe it's the vastness of the stars at night or the depths of unexplored oceans. Maybe it's the way nature recovers once it destroys something like in the case of natural disasters. What if it's the power of a storm? The way the storm generates energy, organizes into a powerful force, then destroys, and just disappears leaving the birds to sing again. Often labels are used for ease of reference, and in this step, God is an easy word to use. If it doesn't work, use a different word!

You may relate to God as Universe, Spirit, Higher Power, Source,

Mother Nature, or something of the like. Connecting to a Higher Power of any identity represents the love, grace, compassion, and forgiveness we all seek and that is available in the divine nature of all these names. Based on where you are in your journey, feel free to interchange your preferred name for the Higher Power that you feel the most connected to. The real invitation is to turn your life over and surrender to the protection, healing, and guidance of that Power.

The fourth step asks us to make a searching and fearless moral inventory of ourselves.

This was the step where things really started to change, and the magic began. I mean, moral inventory? Talk about looking in a mirror! Taking inventory, making a list of who wronged me, was an interesting experience because naturally, I began to realize my role in the relationship. This exercise caused me to take an honest look at my part in the chaos. I could see the messes I had made and saw the casualties along the way.

I saw how my patterns played out and how I harmed others as much as I felt harmed. I saw the impact of my choices and it was hard to look at. This is where I slowly began to push through the past cycles of harmful behaviors and relationships. It took awareness, consistency, and responsibility but over time, I was able to break the chains that kept me cycling in my looping patterns.

I invite and even challenge you to search your past and take a fearless, moral inventory of yourself.

- Who has wronged you?
- What did they do?
- How did you participate in the relationship?
- How did you engage with the wrongdoing?
- How might you have wronged them?

Part of my shifting from victim to survivor included taking responsibility for my actions and reactions. I think it needs to be said: none of us are perfect angels. It doesn't justify someone mistreating you but likely there are behaviors for you to acknowledge as well. This is only if you can recognize that your life has become unmanageable by playing the victim role. There is no power in victimhood. Therefore, you must look at your role in your unhealthy behaviors and relationships. Taking your power back will give you an opportunity to shift the quality of your life.

Step five took step four a bit further: Admit to God, to ourselves, and to another human being the exact nature of our wrongs.

This was a beautifully challenging experience. I had written a list of all those who had wronged me and shared it with my sponsor. This list was a long one. My mom, stepfather, significant others, and friends, it was a list of people from my entire life. It took a lot of time and deep soul searching, but this was the most powerful exercise I had ever done.

I had to explore my past with new lenses. I had to look at each of my relationships—friends and lovers—to see through and beyond my stories. I had to dig into the "why" behind my own destructive ways. I had to admit and own my part.

When it was time to share it with my sponsor, we sat in her backyard by the pool on a sunny afternoon. I was nervous on the inside, but the backyard was so peaceful that it helped me relax. We were surrounded by trees, and the birds were singing.

One by one, I spoke the words of each individual in my life that had hurt me. I cried a few times as I went over the list. It was difficult to write and even harder to read, but I was committed to getting all the way through it and I did. As I spoke out about those who have hurt me, there was a shift, a release.

On a new level, I recognized my part in the relationships. This didn't feel good. Of course, I was sharing all of this with my sponsor in her backyard, but I felt and knew I was being seen and heard by that power greater than me. I know that it is always watching over us, but I see now that I had been out of my mind while I was behaving this way. This was the first time that I was acknowledging what had happened to me and my participation in all of it. This was heavy to describe, yet that weight came off when I shared it all.

After processing and purging all this past pain, she encouraged me to take some time to myself. She gave me some space, I lay on a lawn chair, took a few deep breaths, and closed my eyes. I lay there listening, smelling, and sensing my surroundings, just trying to relax a bit. I felt the warmth of the sun and felt the presence of peace. I was still processing what had just taken place and memories started flashing in my mind. Trying not to slide into a panic, I just pondered and breathed. I began to think about myself with a genuine curiosity. This felt like a self-study type of learning experience. It felt like a second chance, instead of the "new beginning" that I used to chase. I started thinking about how I could have done things differently. I was watching my memories play in my mind and recognizing what had happened in my relationships. Things started to click, and it showed me what I'd never been able to see before. I looked for how I could have changed how I responded, interpreted, and reacted in healthier ways.

This process was powerful for me, and I invite you to give it a try. Be willing to be witnessed in your pain and behavior. Be willing to talk about it. Be willing to be seen for what has happened *to* and *by* you. Being witnessed is a practice that is so effective in the healing process and can't be replaced simply by journaling and keeping it to yourself. It is your willingness to be seen and heard that you finally *feel* seen, heard, and forgiven.

Step six asks us if we are entirely ready to have God remove all these defects of character.

This step caused such a pivotal shift in the quality of my life and relationships. This is where I surrendered my anger and opened myself to change my cycles. I opened fully to God (as I understand him) taking over. He took away my desire to drink, and day by day, as the fog lifted, I was able to see more clearly.

When I looked at my relationships, I saw my cycles. The patterns that I have been referring to for the entirety of this book were not clear to me until sobriety. Once I began the work of taking responsibility, I could see my behaviors in relationships. I saw how they began, carried on, and ended in a very particular way. I saw the give and take in the relationship. I saw how I responded and pushed away.

I recognized that once I felt I was not receiving the affection I needed or wanted, I would start to push or run away. Because I had such a difficult time communicating my feelings, I put up walls and sabotaged the relationship. My default defense mechanism was to hurt before others could hurt me, but I didn't realize how much this pattern hurt me. This was not obvious to me in my youth. I was just doing what I knew. I was surviving as best as I could, but I was certainly causing my own pain and chaos. When I sobered up, this chaos became obvious, and so did the choice to give my life over to God.

I offered control of my life over to him and prayed for him to remove my defects of character. All my previous attempts had placed me deeper in an emotional hole and farther into addiction. This step allowed me to realize my control, and I was willing and ready to give all of it up. I needed something, anything, to work for me. I trusted this path would take me in a healthier direction.

Step seven is humbly asking Him/Her/It to remove our shortcomings.

Asking God to help me change was sometimes hard because initially I didn't want to admit my wrongdoings. This can be true for a lot of us. As I mentioned about victimhood, we are perfect angels in our own eyes. Everyone else is to blame. Everyone else is the cause of our pain, but accepting our own shortcomings is a true sign of strength and healing. It's not always easy or comfortable, but it is always worth it.

The themes of steps six and seven are about surrender and release. The real release is of any illusion of perfection and control. My life had become unmanageable because I refused to acknowledge my shortcomings and weaknesses. It was finally time to surrender to my humanness.

We do our best to maintain a sense of control for most of our lives and it was the Serenity Prayer, prayed a dozen times a day, that helped me move through these two steps of trying to comprehend a power so gracious and loving that he would carry me through my true and lasting recovery.

I offered my Higher Power my life and my shortcomings with it. Without him, I am weak. With him, I can do anything. I know that now.

Step eight instructs us to make a list of all persons we've harmed and become willing to make amends to them all.

This list, much like the first one, set me free in ways I could have never imagined. There were still times I wanted to slip into my victimhood, but I had already pledged to doing everything I was told. I was one hundred percent committed to the program, so I executed this exercise fully.

Admitting that I wronged someone helped me face myself. It helped me practice forgiveness of self, others, and God. When we are hurt so badly in this lifetime, we often need *someone* to blame. It is easy to blame others, it is usually our first response. Oftentimes, we default to blaming ourselves. I did this harshly for most of my life. We can also blame the situation and wish our pasts had gone differently, or that our lives in general were different. I have also experienced and seen people find blame in a God that would let them go through such pain and suffering.

No matter where you find fault, forgiveness is another key to your freedom and peace. Forgiveness is for yourself. Forgiveness does not mean that you forget or excuse the harm done to you, but forgiveness brings you a kind of peace that helps you move forward in life.

Making amends includes stepping up to say that your behavior was a part of the problem. It takes courage and a willingness to come out on the other side of this struggle. I opened my heart to the willingness to make amends and that became my next step.

Step nine instructs us to make direct amends to such people wherever possible, except when to do so would injure them or others.

This was huge. Here, I apologized and asked for forgiveness from those that I had hurt. I did this with a handful of people, but the day I chose to make amends with my husband was incredible and the most memorable.

That day was a sign from beyond. In fact, every day sober, a spiritual presence became clearer and more prominent in my life. Throughout the remainder of this book, I will share a few signs from the other side that are just too synchronistic to overlook, but I want to make note of the way that Source, the Universe, the Divine, or God made their presence and approval known. I felt like I was always being nudged with signs of acknowledgment in my life. This encouraged me greatly. It is what inspired me to finally write my story. I knew I wanted to share the presence of God and how she/he/it will show up in daily life if you are attentive, looking, and listening. He will guide you to your fullest life if you surrender, pay attention, and accept the signs, and my husband and I received a clear sign when I made amends.

We were in our family room in our new home. We moved shortly after I started the program to recovery. We sat on the couch, and I began to apologize for the hurt that I had caused with my drinking and destructive cycles. I took the opportunity to ask for forgiveness and understanding for my actions. I cried my way through my amends and felt so healed by his embrace and acceptance of my apology.

Our dog, a yellow lab, sat at my husband's feet while we talked. At the end, Quaker jumped up in his lap to give him a hug too. It lightened the heavy conversation. It was such a cathartic moment to have a laugh after all those tears.

After a few more moments on the couch, we walked out back for some fresh air. It was a beautiful spring day and when we got outside, we noticed thousands of ladybugs surrounding us. It was breathtaking. Everywhere we looked, there they were. Both pleasantly surprised, we looked at one another, cried, and said we knew something much greater than ourselves was with us. We embraced yet again and simply enjoyed this beautiful sign from God.

I later looked up the spiritual meaning of the ladybug and they represent luck, prosperity, and love. Laughter, excitement, and love are all traits of the ladybug. Where she flies, joy follows.

Researching the ladybug inspired me to appreciate our relationship, marriage, and parenthood. Ray and I have shared so much meaningful love and laughter. At the height of my addiction, I was self-centered because of the effects of the alcohol, but my sobriety helped me get in touch with my heart and feel gratitude again. Admitting my wrongs to Ray and asking for forgiveness was our chance to move forward, forgive, and offer a rebirth to the relationship. Going through this program saved my marriage, and this step healed it.

As you are reading about the steps, I want to continue to encourage you to give them a try. You may not feel the need to be in any organized system or may not specifically be in recovery, but you don't have to be to want to improve your overall quality of life. This is work you can take on if you are ready to clear energetic blocks in your body that keep you bogged down, unhappy, confused, exhausted, resentful, and hopeless. I feel confident in encouraging working the steps to clear anything for you to be living your most fulfilled life. This work is for everyone.

By step ten of the program, anyone going through the process would have done a lot of clean-up work in their life. By this step, the work is focused on maintenance and improvement. Step ten reminds us to continue taking personal inventory and when we are wrong, promptly admitting it.

This step asks us to stay diligent about our patterns and defaults. It is an invitation to watch for the mistakes we often make and choose a new behavior. It is important to recognize how we wrong others, admit our wrongs, and admit what we have done when we slip up and fall. This shift is about being accountable for our actions. This is where we can actually make a change in our life patterns because we choose a new response. I will share more about this in the next chapter because learning to love myself enough to let things go and choose a new response changed the rest of my life and relationships.

One of my favorite steps became number eleven, because besides prayer and naps, I used meditation to get much closer to my Higher Power. Step eleven asks us to seek God through prayer and meditation. It invites us to improve our conscious contact with God, as we understand him/her/it, praying only for knowledge of that will for us and the power to carry it out.

Since working the program, and for years now, I have grown to love meditation to connect directly to my understanding of God. There are many types and styles of meditation, and it's important to find one that works for you. People believe that prayer is talking to the Source and meditating is listening for Source to talk to us. There are guided meditations, seated, walking, one-pointed focus, meditations with beads (rosary/mala), in nature, in sacred places, with music, without, and the list goes on. Find what speaks to you. When I drop into meditation, I have a full experience of leaving my body and entering another realm of existence. It is a magical experience, and I am so grateful for it. I feel like I can sense Spirit within and outside of me, and my guidance becomes clear. Learning how to meditate, then consistently doing it, is what made step twelve so natural for me.

Step twelve speaks of having had a spiritual awakening as the result of these steps. I felt that was occurring in the most natural and divine way and it invigorated my passion for life. I would drop into my meditations and receive clear guidance of what there was for me to do as a child and light of God here on Earth. As I embraced meditating, I found a whole new chamber of spirituality opened for me. I began to tune into signs and coincidences, realizing that Spirit was at play, presenting these subtleties just for me. I felt divinely inspired and chosen. I truly live in these blessings daily. Step twelve invites us to carry the message of the steps to alcoholics, and to practice these principles in all our affairs.

I began to do that day in and day out. It started at meetings and leaked into my community. We were always encouraged to be a living example of God's will and I was happy to walk that path. As this book continues, I will share much more about how beautifully life has unfolded since formally completing the program. Of course, the work is never done. We wake up every day as an alcoholic, until one day, maybe we don't feel like an alcoholic anymore; still, we walk the steps. We must continue the work of routines, the meetings as long as they serve us, our medicine of prayer and meditation, and staying connected through community where we can serve others. This daily work took me and my life in a new direction.

23

Learning to Love Myself

I remember when I turned forty and I was off to a celebratory dinner with friends. I was in the car on the way to the restaurant and I told my friend that I was so afraid of getting older because I had relied on my looks my whole life. I felt to my core that I was going to lose the only thing I *thought* I had to offer the world. I felt like I was nothing else, just a shell of a human being. This moment was monumental.

I was a year into the program and the shift was occurring. I was developing a strong relationship with my inner self. I was coming to understand and *accept* that I did have more to offer.

For most of my life, I thought I was stupid. It is only in the clarity of sobriety that I realize it was because I lived in a fog while drinking every day. I never knew my passions or interests because of my quest to drink. It was a huge distraction. It is for many people who don't realize what an inhibitor it is. Drinking suppressed and dulled all I had to offer in life.

It was a pivotal time in my life when I began to know and love myself. Again, I had to convince myself that that was okay.

At the core of healing, you must love yourself before you can love others fully and then receive love. The highest vibration is love.

God is love and wants us to all love ourselves.

Now, going back to the first time I said those words, I felt a number of emotions. Relief, elation, embarrassment, awe, happiness, thankfulness, and belief for the first time that everything was going to be okay.

It got easier to say. My love for myself grew and it began to feel natural, as it should. Loving ourselves can feel selfish but it is the greatest gift we can give to ourselves. It is also one of the greatest gifts we can give others. When we love ourselves, we are available to give and receive love in a relationship.

When you start to love yourself, there is a light within you that begins to grow—a fullness and joy that is hard to put into words. Never feel shame or let anyone shame you for saying out loud that you love yourself. God equals love and you equal love. Love is the core of pure joy and that is what we all deserve and is our purpose in this life.

The first time I said I loved myself was an "aha" moment for me. It was in a meeting. It felt so foreign to say those words. I had hated myself for so long that it felt egocentric to even feel that way, but I was also willing to forge a new path. Self-hatred and judgment hadn't worked all those years. It seemed worth a shot.

When I said it out loud in a meeting for the first time, I felt like everyone was looking at me. I figured they were judging me as if I was speaking from a place of ego. This made me uncomfortable, but no more uncomfortable than how I had been struggling for so long. I was willing to keep practicing this new self-love, which is in reference to prioritizing my well-being more than loving myself as if I were perfect.

Afterward, I told myself that it was okay. I wanted to get healthy and loving myself was an essential part of that. I had to care about my body, mind, heart, soul, and life for it to get better. I think that every time I said it, I believed it a little bit more. I never believed it a *lot* more at any one time, but my continued work with the steps, my constant prayer, my devoted meditation, and my slow and gradual progress had me thinking, "I guess I do love myself! I am willing to love myself."

"I love myself enough to get healthy. I love my family. I love my life. I want it all to keep getting better, and I am getting better. Maybe I do love myself!" And I kept getting better. Day after week after month, I kept getting better.

Something else that kept getting better were my actions and reactions. Part of my challenge was to let things go and change my responses to events and people. I was raised in an angry environment. Most of the people in my family had a temper and everyone communicated by yelling and fighting. It was what I knew. For so long, my reactions and responses were to drink and fight. Drink and yell. Drink and work. Drink and criticize. Drink and drive. When it got to that last one, I knew it couldn't go on, but arriving at that point caused me to look at all the other behaviors associated with my drinking.

Once I decided to shift from victim to survivor, I had to learn how to pause before going straight into my victim role and start drinking and fighting. It was so familiar and easy to take that route. It was much more challenging for me to stop when I felt confronted and checked in with myself.

Even well into my recovery and new life, I remember a time when I was sitting around a table of fifteen of the most successful women in their respective industries and wondering how I got there. I remember that even though I had earned a spot at that table, I still questioned my belonging. I certainly questioned my worthiness when one of the women called my newly launched television show a "hobby."

A younger Marci, a drinking Marci, would have not only been highly offended, but she also would have gotten pissed off, maybe even told her off, and held a grudge forevermore. Instead, I went back to my hotel room, shed some tears, felt my reactive painful feelings, and then took a moment to inquire with myself, "Why am I upset about this?"

I knew I was upset because she had poked at a soft spot of my belief in myself at that stage of my recovery and developing business.

She highlighted for me that I was afraid to ask for money because I felt unworthy of compensation. Because of this new awareness provided by a painful comment, I hired a content producer, and she began making sales left and right for my show.

It was a huge sign of progress to not spiral into self-doubt, rage, and hatred after a trigger like that. Because I learned and decided to let things go and change my response, I was able to have more breakthroughs than breakdowns. I was able to turn triggers into triumphs.

This took a lot of practice, but the self-love that I was learning in the 12-Step program taught me that I love myself enough to step back and take another look at every situation.

Every day in every way, I got better at loving myself, letting things go, and responding with love. I let my Higher Power work through me and let God show me the beauty in all things. I knew I wasn't driving the bus anymore. I was allowed to release my grip on control and just enjoy the ride and the views; the views got better with each passing day.

Over the course of my recovery, I have been given *plenty* of opportunities to pause and let go of anger. I could tell endless stories of times I have felt wronged or betrayed, even after getting sober, but the difference was within me, not outside of me.

I want you to know this as you commit to living a better, fuller life. Life is still challenging. People are still challenging. You will still be challenged, often. What changes is how you respond to the challenges life hands you. Instead of flying off the handle and picking up the bottle (or whatever has taken over your life), you can choose a new response. You can set those things down, come to center with yourself, and inquire about why Source would have you face this kind of challenge. You can seek and find a lesson in these opportunities.

It is truly hard work. It's the hardest work I've ever done, but my life is full of abundance because of it. Once I stopped masking who I was with alcohol, I started to blossom. I found happiness when I began reconnecting with the Marci I lost so many years ago. This made way for an entirely new life experience and not spiraling out of control every time I was confronted afforded me a chance to create forward momentum in my life.

It was challenging to love myself after all that I had been through and done. Letting go of things I had held onto for decades was about as comfortable as being awake during an operation. Changing my responses took a lot of failed attempts. I wasn't perfect at this work. I still am not.

But I am committed. I have vowed to myself and to God to be a light of hope. I promised myself to use my gifts to the best of my ability to help others move forward with their healing journey. I swore I would do everything within my power to help people the way that people have helped me, and I want to show up for you in that way.

I want to encourage you to take on the work of loving yourself. I challenge you to look in the mirror after this chapter and announce "I love myself" five times, maybe more, if you can stand to. I challenge you to love yourself because you cannot love your life or anyone in it if you are unwilling to give yourself that love first.

Once I was clear-minded and emotionally sober, I was able to start recognizing my gifts. As we continue into the last section of this book, I will start sharing how my life opened and developed with my sobriety journey.

It gets better, my friend, and as we move into Part Four, I will show you the many ways that it does. Let's proceed into our future.

PART 4

Seeing the Signs

24

Seeing the Signs

Learning to love myself started a new trend where I started to develop levels of courage I had never experienced before. Sure, I had gone for big promotions, got the guy, or booked the modeling gig, but that was when I relied on liquid courage. When I learned how to love myself, I took steps in alignment with my faith and my true value.

This opened a whole new world of possibility for me.

Loving myself, changing my responses, and shifting my relationships took years of practice and commitment. In all honesty, it is a life-long journey. I am especially proud of the changes I made early in my sobriety journey. As I continued to walk the path, my courage increased, and I took more and more leaps of faith as time went on.

The same month that I had gotten sober, we were in the process of selling our house to move essentially across the street. We did not want to move, but a new land development project forced us to relocate. The neighborhood was going to be changing so it was for the best, but it wasn't something we wanted. This was a very trying time for me and every day required a conscious effort not to choose alcohol. Talk about stress! I learned to rely on my newfound trust and surrender and the knowledge that I had greater power around me, on my side, and looking out for me. When the house didn't sell for almost a year, I remember walking over to it and stopping to pray.

I walked through the bare halls and recalled good and bad times. I ran my hands over some of the surfaces and remembered cooking and gathering with friends. I looked over my babies' rooms, who were no longer babies. I think the house was not selling because I was not ready to let it go. I loved it for many reasons. When I stopped to pray, I asked Source to please cleanse the house for the next owner to have a fresh start in this beautiful space. I spoke out loud that I was truly ready to let the old me and my old life completely go, and to continue along this healthy path. I added my gratitude for all the good that continued to come my way. The very next week, the house sold.

I was taken aback when my husband gave me the news. It seemed like I just asked God to help us sell it and he did. Getting sober and moving were two major life transitions at once, and I felt like God took the house right off my plate when I asked him to. This caught and held my attention. It was one of those lessons in surrender for me. I knew there was a plan for me, and I felt like he communicated that clearly when he helped the house sell.

He communicated even more clearly a week later while I was sitting in our new backyard with my feet in our pool, and hundreds, literally *hundreds*, of dragonflies surrounded me. The specific symbol of the dragonfly in my life at that time was the perfect sign I needed from the other side.

The dragonfly represents transformation, adaptability, and self-realization. It represents mental and emotional maturity and understanding the deeper meaning of life. This was happening to me, and it calmed my nerves while I was in my new life.

I think the stress I was feeling was the anticipation of the unknown but there was an unmistakable message in the presence of those dragonflies. I got this overwhelmingly clear message that everything was going to be fine and with tears in my eyes, I exhaled a huge sigh of relief. I felt completely heard and held in that moment, surrounded by God, love, and peace. I knew then that more surrender was in store for me.

That day, I accepted dragonflies as my sign from God and the Universe to represent that I was on the right path. I now look for my sign when I seek confirmation of a decision. It also sometimes shows up when I am not seeking it and it brings a smile to my face and makes my heart skip a beat. Whenever I recognize the dragonfly in my life, I am more aware of the presence of God.

Dragonflies move with elegance and grace. Symbolically, this represented the true transformation in my life. I have become more elegant and graceful in my sobriety and spirituality. As a daily reminder, I wear a beautiful dragonfly necklace that Ray gave to me in my first year of sobriety. It is part of my branding in my current business, and dragonflies show up often in my life as a reminder.

25

DUI Sentencing

I needed signs of guidance during these different growth periods of my life when I was taking leaps of faith into my future. After my DUI, I took a serious inventory of my life and knew it was time to take a step back from my career to focus on my relationships and family. Although challenging, it was time to discover myself without alcohol, but first, I had to formally end that chapter of my life.

It was time to go to court for my DUI sentencing. It was March of 2016, and I was about six months sober and already felt like a completely different person from the one who was arrested. I was consistently going to AA and working the steps, but it was time to face the consequences of my actions. I was a nervous wreck.

The day before my hearing, I was praying that I would receive the minimum. I was stressed and as many of us do, I started asking God to fix it for me. I was on my knees, in tears. If I got the maximum sentencing, I was looking at a year with no license and possibly a breathalyzer installed in my car. Being a mom, I couldn't imagine being without a license to get my kids to school or their activities. I was the primary caretaker, and as many moms know, one of the job titles includes taxi driver.

I was struggling with fear, shame, and disgust about how I ended up in that position but there I was, back in the midst of my terrible decision. I was proud of where I was going with my sobriety, but I still had great shame. As I knelt there that evening and prayed for God to take it all away, I felt disingenuous. I expected to face the consequences of what I had done, but I was afraid of paying such a hefty penalty.

When I realized I was asking my Higher Power to fix the situation, I changed my prayer immediately. I changed my narrative and asked Source to give me what he thought I needed to learn from this experience. "God grant me the serenity to accept the things I cannot change, courage to change the things I can, and wisdom to know the difference." I prayed for wisdom and serenity instead of an easy way out. The prayer caused a shift within me. I felt at peace and trusted that whatever the outcome was, I would accept it with grace. I knew God had me and would show me what was necessary for my healing.

That next morning, I went to court with my lawyer, husband, and sponsor. I sat in the courtroom full of nerves, fear, and sadness. I sat there just wondering what would happen. The judge walked in, and I went to the front of the courtroom.

Moments later, I saw the police officer that arrested me walk in. My heart dropped.

Our eyes met and a flood of memories from that day came back. I felt a rush of heat run up my neck and the sides of my cheeks. I felt in trouble, like when called to the principal's office. I felt so uneasy, but I still tried to smile at him. I was hoping he would feel my energy of remorse and see the healing in my eyes.

My lawyer was going for the lowest sentencing but told me it would probably not happen. I had blown double the alcohol limit when this man pulled me over. For that alone, I didn't think I stood a chance at a minimal sentence. Nonetheless, my lawyer presented it.

The only way for that to work was that the arresting officer had to agree to the terms. The sentencing began and my lawyer laid out our case for the judge. He explained what we wanted and my recovery efforts. I stood there standing tall and very still, doing my best to look attentive and apologetic at the same time, relying on faith and Spirit.

The judge looked at me and I looked back, holding eye contact. I was nervous and uneasy, but I wanted to show my genuine regret and desire to reform. After a few moments' gaze, he asked me if I was done drinking. In the sincerest way, I looked him in the eyes and with my whole body, mind, and spirit, said "Yes!"

I wanted him to *feel* my truth. I was done with my old ways. From behind the bench, he said he knew I was telling him the truth because of how I looked him in the eyes. "Most don't," he said. "They are usually just saying what they think I want to hear." I was starting to feel more optimistic about how this might turn out. The knot in my stomach was beginning to untangle.

The judge spoke with the police officer, who had just watched the whole exchange, and he too, agreed to the lowest sentencing. I received three months with no license, and I did not have to put a breathalyzer in my car. I could have collapsed with relief. I could hardly believe it. I knew at that moment I had assistance from beyond and it gave me what I needed. I was doing the work and I was given the consequence that I needed.

This whole situation was a huge sign from Source that he was listening and was in control of my path. It was also a reminder to continuously surrender to his plan. The Universe is truly listening, but we must do our part as well. We are co-creators and for God's will to be done on Earth, we must do our part. I had truly turned my will over to God and my life was on a much better path. I became even more willing to follow the guidance and I stayed on the lookout for more signs.

26

Virgin Mary Messages

In December of that same year, we took our annual trip to the Bahamas, and I received a clear communication during a tarot card reading. I enjoy the guidance of card readings because I feel that they give precise messages to consider and incorporate into our lives. While the message in this reading seemed pretty specific, its manifestation was unmistakable.

"The Virgin Mary is trying to give you signs," the woman reading said. "Look for the signs. Look for roses."

Look for the roses... I thought for the rest of the day. I remember sort of feeling in a meditative daze as I walked through my day, wondering what specifically the Virgin Mother Mary might have to say to me.

Just a few, short days later, I got that message loud and clear from Mother Mary. We were on a boat surrounded by turquoise water in the Bahamas. I was on the boat thinking to myself about looking for signs. I was wondering how I could see the signs I was hoping for surrounded by water.

When I looked down, the bag I was carrying from the vacation rental caught my eye. It had a picture of a woman surrounded by roses. The roses caught my eye immediately and when I saw the woman in the picture, I felt this powerful connection with her. What was so unmistakable about this sign was the message underneath it: "love yourself the way you are." My jaw practically fell to the floor.

I had spent that whole year learning to love myself again, and there I was, getting a perfectly clear message that I was on the right path. The Universe, God, and even the Virgin Mary bring you *exactly* what you need to keep you on your journey. Yes, it took me by surprise, but it also felt like the familiar feeling of being guided. Once I picked my jaw up, the bag with the saying on it brought a smile to my face, a tear to my eye, and put a pep in my step. I hugged the frame gently, holding it to my heart. I was grateful to receive *such* a divine message in a personal way. I knew to keep walking down the path of self-love.

I spent a few more months into 2017 focusing on my family and relationships. I was also starting to feel ready to go back to work. I was not pursuing acting, but I went to gigs that my agent booked for me. I did a photoshoot here and an infomercial there. I wasn't too sure I wanted to get back into the industry, but I could feel something brewing in my heart.

27

Ready to Give It Up

Around March, I had heard of a friend who was building his own garage recording and sound studio. He had a green screen and other production equipment. When I went to see it for the first time, I had a buzz of excitement from seeing everything so familiar. I was back in a studio, a place I hadn't realized felt like home in its own special way.

Being in that space, I felt guided to harness my experience in television and use what I knew to give back to my community. This seemed like a perfect opportunity—the physical manifestation of what had been bubbling within me. After a few conversations, I offered to help my friend find clients. I connected with content creators, show hosts, and sound producers to use his studio for their projects. Not long after getting started, I had a project of my own in mind.

I had the idea of a talk show. I shared with him that I could find guests within the community, we could find a host, and we could feature them and their businesses. We were both excited, so I thought. I had brought in clients for his studio and sponsors for our show. We were moving ahead to get everything set up. When I brought in my first guest, it became very clear to me that we had different ideas in mind and wanted to take the project in different directions.

I was still early in my healing, sobriety, and spirituality, so there were times when I felt angry about how it was or wasn't going. I felt slighted and wronged (back into victimhood), and it was easy for me to choose a bad attitude about it all. There were times I wanted to kick, scream, and fight (old patterns). There were times that I reacted negatively and later, felt shame, wishing I had walked away to process my feelings first.

I eventually did walk away from that friend and his studio, but not before getting a clear lesson. Throughout my time in the program, and after many signs from the other side, I knew there was a plan and a path for me. However, I didn't always like when that plan included lessons about things not going my way, or how I envisioned them. I knew Spirit hit me with some disappointment to push me that much further outside of my comfort zone. These were challenging lessons that humbled me and threw fuel on the fire of my passion. I had gotten far enough into our project and my healing journey to realize that I wanted to make a difference by giving back to my community.

While things were falling apart at the studio, things were also falling apart with acting. My career was mostly lackluster and a bit of a drag. I wasn't fully into how it was going, and I was feeling ready to be done.

I was sure I was done one day in June of 2017 when I had a bad infomercial shoot. Everything seemed to go wrong, and I didn't have any energy for that anymore. It was a series of mishaps and challenges, and it was a terrible day overall. I felt defeated, and I was ready to call it quits. The old me would have turned to drinking, but the new me chalked it up to a bad day at the office. I went home and put my work to work. I thought to myself, "Okay, I had a bad day, but how do I want to *react* to this bad day?"

Instead of drinking, I went to bed. In the middle of the night, I woke up thinking about it and made a pros and cons list of giving up my acting career. After making that list, I decided to call my agent in the morning and let her know I was done.

I rolled over with a sense of relief knowing that I was done with modeling and acting. As I did that, I felt something sort of sharp and picked it up. Wondering what it was, I sat up quickly and turned the light on to check it out. Oddly, and very out of nowhere, there was my modeling business card, in my bed: the card that I hadn't used in over a year!

I think it is important to note that my stack of business cards was neatly in a drawer of my office desk downstairs, nowhere near my bedroom. I didn't work up there and there was no explanation for how that card got into my bed. It was just too out of the ordinary to ignore. I felt a rush of awareness come over me, knowing that I wouldn't give up being in front of the camera and on screen.

I decided right then and there that I wouldn't give up. I think that "they" decided that long before me, but the path had become visible to me at that time. I knew I would keep pursuing my career, but now, guided by the will of my team of angels. I surrendered, yet again, to a plan much greater than mine. I knew I would use my television skills and experience to give back to the community the way I'd planned. I did not know what that would look like, but I surrendered and let God guide me.

28

A Show is Born

A seed was planted when working with my friend at the previous studio. I had thought of a talk show but figured it would be a talk show that someone else hosted. Soon enough, I began to ask myself the question, "Why not me?"

I had never hosted a talk show, but the desire became overwhelmingly strong. It was clear to me that this was God's plan. He was guiding me with these thoughts about the show and they were developing every day. They would not go away and kept getting stronger. I no longer had the connection with the studio, but I thought to myself, "Why can't I do it on my own?"

It began to make more sense to me that I could—and should—do it on my own. I had a guest, my first guest from the other studio, and a strong desire. It was when Facebook Live had just become popular, so I figured I would just go live with my friend who is an entrepreneur and share what she does with the community. She agreed, I propped up the phone at her home, and we went live for the first time!

I felt so invigorated in that moment, and it continued to grow from there. I was still not sure of the vision, but I remained open, looking for signs along the way. It became clear one day at a vendor party. I knew I was going to interview the vendors but wasn't sure of my angle. That day, the message came to me strongly. A loud voice in my head said, "you will give entrepreneurs and nonprofits a voice," and my vision was born.

That day, I was spotlighting the vendors at the show and giving them coverage of what they were doing and selling. It was such a hit. The vendors loved it, the viewers watching loved it, and I was getting great feedback. Immediately, people were asking to be featured, and I was gently forced to consider exactly what I was doing and how I would be doing it.

Within a few days, I had written a formal mission statement and came up with a name for my new talk show, *Coffee with Marci*. I still have my original brainstorming saved in my notes on my phone. "My mission is to spread information and inspiration through my interviews with entrepreneurs, doctors, and healers working in mind, body, and spirit. I hope to create awareness around what they do for the community and how they were inspired to become entrepreneurs."

My idea for the show was strongly built on a foundation of service. I wanted it to be equally helpful for guests and viewers. The show was centered around the guests and their services, but my viewers' lives were a major priority for me. I knew I wanted this show to be about the community and making a positive contribution.

I wanted to reach a diverse audience and provide different topics. This was true then when I started *Coffee with Marci*, and it is true still today, with this book and my other work in the world. Anything I offer is to help people heal, learn, change their lives for the better, and tap into helpful resources. I want to share the light of hope and practical how-tos for living a fulfilling life.

In my work, I primarily focus on encouraging and empowering women to connect with themselves and find their passion. I set originally out to reach women in their thirties and beyond, to encourage, nurture, and inspire them. I focused on women like me who may also struggle with aging, family, and career. I wanted to serve the mothers who have found their passion after having children. I wanted to encourage the women who left the corporate world to start a business, something that they had dreamt about doing, but never thought was possible.

I once heard, "In life, we learn what we came to teach." I wanted to teach the women who are where I once was and let them know there is life beyond their current struggle. I wanted to help them wake up to their subconscious superpowers. I believe in women thriving and I believe we can all get there together.

In addition to helping women, I also wanted to help families. As a sexual abuse survivor, I masked my pain for years. I coped in unhealthy ways, and it caused a lot of suffering in and around me. This started in childhood and shaped the entire path and trajectory of my life. I struggled for years longer than "necessary." I use quotations because I know that my Higher Power, Source, Spirit took me down that path to arrive right here, right now, *and* I am committed to helping families get healthy much sooner than mine ever did. I wanted to help others who have gone or are going through hardships. We all have a story and are affected by trauma in one way or another. I wanted to positively impact viewers by addressing these topics on the show.

When it came to helping families, I hoped to inspire parents to connect more deeply with their children. I wanted to give children a voice through sharing my story. I tried to catch the attention of parents and invite them to focus on the well-being of their children, to look and listen beyond the surface of everyday life. We are our children's guardians and advocates, and it is up to us to support their development. I felt a deep sense of responsibility as an adult to care for all children, not just my own.

For this reason, I had the idea to feature many health professionals from doctors to healers to counselors and therapists, even lawyers, and more. I believed strongly in the medical field. I also believed strongly in holistic healing and want to offer a wide array of information and resources to my audience. It is often normalized in Western culture to mask internal issues with medications, or simply suppress and ignore pain and negative emotions. I am committed to getting to the bottom of the topics of depression, addiction, learning, and healing by hosting experts in fields, and also by giving voice to personal stories. I wanted to offer my audience new information they may have never been exposed to. I think it is important to have professionals with a variety of modalities on the show to bring these issues to the forefront and potentially offer a new perspective and healthy alternative. We address them in hopes that true healing can begin treatment of the source, not the symptom.

Whether the viewer was a parent, grandparent, aunt, uncle, or whomever, this information could help both the individual and the family unit. I knew this is what I wanted to offer my community.

When I thought about my guests being on the show, I wanted to offer them value for their appearance. I wanted to put a different spin on traditional marketing by featuring the business and sharing value for the viewer. I noticed long ago how a good amount of brilliant small business owners were not tech-savvy, and I didn't think that meant they should lose out on business in the online space in today's digital world. I designed my show to feature them online to get them more coverage and exposure. This excited them as much as it excited me to share their work with my virtual audience.

Not only was this meant to highlight local vendors for service, but this show was also intended to be filled with hope for viewers looking for guidance and inspiration of their own to follow their dreams. My hope was, and is, to ignite individuals to follow their passions, grow as people, connect with those in the community, and learn from others' successes and failures.

My guests have made it through trials and triumphs and want others to know they are not alone in their challenges. I wanted to offer my guests an opportunity to share how they reinvented themselves to become who they are now. The platform I built is dynamic because we offered real help to real people in real-time.

I noticed the viewers liked it because it was organic, real, and more down-to-earth than regular network TV, and the guests liked it because they felt more directly connected to the audience. Viewers were inspired by hearing others' success stories and guests were eager to share.

Because of this, the show gained notoriety quickly and the whole idea got more serious as time progressed.

I smile with joy about how it all started at the vendor show, and I recall recording my first few formal interviews with my phone propped up against a stack of books. The popularity of the show grew overnight, and I developed it piece by piece. Next, I got a ring light and a tripod and started getting more organized every day. People were requesting to be on the show left and right. I could barely keep up with the demand, and I had to grow quickly, so I got a production team and have been evolving year after year.

My leap of faith in loving myself as I am has turned into growing a mission and message. I had to sprint to stay with the pace of the show and I have been enjoying the process. When I surrendered to the will of God, he swept me up and took me down a path I couldn't predict. My healing journey has become an offering back to the world. I wanted to help any and all heal and thrive, and because I did, I was guided, protected, and supported in every step.

29

The Feather Under My Foot

The notoriety that *Coffee with Marci* gained so quickly was a fun rush of excitement. After that impromptu live launch, I began quickly scheduling interviews with new guests. They were amazing interviews, and I loved every minute of it. Because the interviews were so helpful for business owners, I kept getting booked.

Then, in October of that year, I had my first in-person event, and I had an audience, a following. It was a fundraiser fashion show, and I was pretty nervous about it. I had gotten used to my structured interviews so this would be a bit different. When I went live at that very first vendor show, I was going with the flow. I had a blast but had very little expectation for how it would go.

No one was putting any sort of pressure on me, but I felt a certain sense of pride in what I had created and felt like I was stepping even further outside of my comfort zone to take it to the next level. I had butterflies most of the day leading up to the event, and then, there it was, a sign.

I was rushing to get ready. I got my hair and makeup done professionally. I was petrified by the time I was all done up and ready and could barely catch my breath. Just as I opened the car door and stepped foot inside, there was a beautiful white feather on my floorboard. A sense of relief rushed over me.

Immediately, I knew my angels were with me. At this point in my recovery, I was meditating daily and praying to my guides for signs. Feathers are traditionally a sign of hope and spiritual growth. I stopped briefly to appreciate the moment. I felt the presence of my guides in and around me.

For the moment, I didn't have to rush, so I didn't. I slowed down, took a deep breath, and drove off with a sense of peace surrounding me. As you can expect, the event went fine. The night was wonderful, and the show was another hit. I knew I was offering something special to our community and it inspired me to keep going.

PART 5

Breaking the Cycles

30

Learning to See the Signs

I would like to teach you something that I didn't grasp for the longest time: we are *always* tapped into the love of God and the Universe, whether we realize it or not. It is up to us to allow that connection. Regardless of how open we are to it, our angels, guides, loved ones that have crossed over, whatever spiritual beings or beliefs you have, and God always have our back. We are consistently being guided and we can access that information and inspiration anytime we desire. We must choose to get more involved to be able to notice the many messages coming through. We often must eliminate the distractions, disbelief, fear, and doubt that get in the way. Negative emotions and behaviors obstruct our connection with the divine and this can become detrimental to fulfilling our purpose and God's will.

There is a very small, underdeveloped part of me that has known this truth all along. I have always felt the power within me, but I have not always used it for the highest good. In my youth, I knew how to access that attraction power to gain attention or get what I wanted. I knew that my power changed the energy of a room, but I didn't always harness it in positive ways.

This is an important awareness that we must come to respect. When I became sober, I felt this power, and I may even call it *grace*, being restored within me. It is not directly *my* or *your* power, it is the power that creates worlds. It is the power of the Universe. It is the grace of God. It is the strength of oneness of all things and this level of anything is meant to be used with care and intention.

When we are sloppy, lazy, distracted, or selfish with this power, our life becomes unmanageable. We tend to lack focus, direction, or purpose, and may find ourselves led astray or veering off. We may also end up chasing things for temporary satisfaction that are not fulfilling in the long run because they are not for the highest good of all. The material things we tend to idolize or prioritize in this physical realm are lost when we die.

Therefore, taking inventory of our actions, behaviors, relationships, and path is vital to our sustainability. Our longevity is reliant upon the quality of the use of that power within us. When we use that power selfishly, we deteriorate. That leads to burnout and spinout. When we use that power to lift others up, make the world a better place, and allow for Spirit to move through us, we find ourselves in an upward spiral of evolution and contribution.

Once I got sober, redirected my focus, harnessed my power, and centered my life around spirituality, I felt energized and inspired to do the work I am now doing. I have felt guided, and it is through my healing that I have the clarity to pursue the guidance I have received. I am still so present to the power I hold within. When I drop into meditation, I find myself directly connected with God and Spirit. I get a buzz of excitement throughout my body and feel as if I am Him and He is me. Sometimes, while deep into meditation, I forget I even have a body.

I feel like God is moving me in life. Daily, I am tapping into that connection to know my next move. I am using this awareness and grace to make a difference in the world and give a voice to other changemakers. I share all of this because you have this invitation, too.

You have grace and power to channel and elevate the vibration of the planet and Universe. With so much noise, influence, and distraction in today's world, we need more emotionally sober people radiating the grace and power of the divine. It is how we will collectively heal the planet, including its people.

31

The "How" of Staying Sober

I often wanted to know *how* to raise my vibration. Especially in that first year of getting sober, I didn't always feel like I had reliable tools for getting *and* staying away from alcohol, so I want to provide a list of some of my favorite sober strategies, which I picked up from my 12-Step program and other programs along the way. This is the list that I defaulted to when I felt my light dimming. I have shared some of these throughout the book, but some of them are worth repeating because I needed to be reminded dozens of times before they stuck with me.

- Move a muscle, change a thought—as I have shared, this one stopped me from drinking quite a few times. When you get up and get active, your focus is immediately shifted.

- Have a gratitude box—write something you are grateful for each day. This does not have to be anything monumental. It could be that you woke up that day. It could be something that made you smile, or anything really. What is especially fun is making an event out of the day you open that box once a year to acknowledge a year's worth of gratitude.

- Meditate—a personal favorite. If you are a beginner, you can look up guided meditations online. You can sit still to music or silence, even take a walk in nature to quiet your mind. Meditation is one of the most powerful spiritual tools we have and remember, practice, practice, practice! We all start somewhere, and it is usually in a place of confusion. Just keep practicing.

- Talking, and sharing your truth—this can be challenging at first. Depending on your past, vulnerability may feel unsafe for you. This practice can set you free from hiding in pain and isolation. If you need to start with a professional like a therapist or a counselor, so be it! Sharing your truth will absolutely change your life.

- Journaling—this one is powerful and can be quite challenging to stay consistent with. I encourage you to start a thirty-day journaling commitment and see how your life transforms. There is something magical about getting all those thoughts and feelings stored in your body out onto paper. (There is an opportunity to begin journaling at the end of this book.)

- Turning to your Higher Power—this is a humbling experience. Turning to your Higher Power represents the honesty you have with yourself that you don't have it all figured out. It is you finally asking for the help and guidance you need. In case no one ever told you, ask and it is given. Turn to your Higher Power and ask for that which can save your life.

- Giving back—this has become a cornerstone in my life. Giving back helps others and it also gives you a sense of self-worth. Talk about a win-win. Giving back helps us to feel good, like we do make a difference, and sometimes we need a real-life reminder that we are important in order to keep showing up. It is okay that we need that reminder, and we can give ourselves that experience by giving back.

- Spending time with others—isolating is one of the fastest ways to lose ourselves and our connection to the divine.

Spending time with others keeps us tethered to this physical realm and reality. When we get trapped in our heads and stay in our room, we can lose touch and ultimately lose our purpose and love for life. Addiction has its strongest hold on us when we allow ourselves to isolate.

- Call someone each day—close to spending time with others, calling someone each day keeps us in action around connection and service. Remember, sometimes you need the call and sometimes, the person you call needs you. You can be a blessing to hear from.

- Nap, a lot—well, nap as much as you think you need—but I will never forget when I heard Abraham Hicks say, "napping stops the momentum of negative thought." This was a lightbulb moment for me. I was ready to change my negative thoughts and napping helped me stop that train and restore myself back to hope and create momentum in the positive direction.

- Pray for guidance—similar to going to your Higher Power, specifically remember prayer is a valuable tool to have in your toolbox. I could write a whole other book about how many times prayer has worked, almost immediately, for me. Praying is just a conversation with your Higher Power, asking specifically for support and guidance, it is surrendering to a God that moves mountains. Always remember the power of prayer, it is the stuff of miracles.

- Communicate—in relationships. When we enter a space of communication, we are opening an opportunity for understanding. Communication is a chance to connect in relationships that cannot be achieved otherwise. The only way communication works is through talking and listening. Listen to hear, instead of listening to respond. It is through true, open, and honest communication that we can resolve hardships in a relationship.

- Try to think of the other person's perspective or feelings—

when we struggle with emotional intoxication, anger, rage, hate, frustration, and bitterness thinking beyond our own experience can be challenging. We are focused on how hurt we are, and we want relief. Thinking of the other person can take us outside of ourselves in a way that gives perspective and alters the experience altogether. This shift can help us sober up quickly and reach resolution.

- Don't try to be right—having to be right can be a toxic trait that stunts our growth. If you look at "How might I be wrong?" or "How might I be perceiving this incorrectly?" the answers could give you a pathway to a new perspective that sets you free from the imprisonment of your pain.

- Admit when you are wrong and apologize—this one is a real sign of growth and can be a total game-changer. When we go back in life to clean up the messes we made when we were fighting for our rightness, we can correct behaviors and restore valuable relationships. Also, apologizing is self-forgiveness for taking a misstep. You can never forgive yourself enough. In the eyes of God, you are always forgiven. There is no need to punish yourself for mistakes made. Clean them up and move forward.

- Remind yourself that it's not all about you—shocker, I know. The Universe doesn't revolve around us and honestly, what a relief! When you remember that it's not all about you, you will remember that people's words, actions, and reactions are not about you, and you can practice more grace. Also, when it's not all about you, the pressure to be perfect can go away and you can live in grace for yourself, too.

- Listen—pay attention. Slow down. Watch the world go on without your input. This is when you realize it is not all about you. You get to participate but you also get to choose how you participate, and when you listen, you will gain a better idea of how to participate positively.

- Stay in a solution-based frame of mind—a problem-based

mind sees and creates problems. A solution-based mind sees and creates more solutions. It is as simple as that, and since there is always a problem or solution available, you get to choose between them.

- Say thank you and think of things you're grateful for every day—gratitude is the ultimate quality of life hack. It is an instant mood booster. Gratitude breeds more gratitude so on top of your gratitude jar, walk through your day focused on every little thing you can be grateful for. The list is endless.

As I have been sharing the evolution of my talk show, it has felt important to share some of the literal practices that kept positive momentum rolling in my life. I was not doing these things in my television career. I was not doing them in the early stages of marriage and motherhood, either. I was not thinking, talking, and behaving this way in my relationships before sobriety and because of that, I was falling apart in many ways. Falling all the way apart in my addiction was necessary to be put back together.

All these strategies I shared helped me put down the drink and maintain my healing journey, yet regardless of your issue (or even if there's no issue, you may just want to get more present in your life!), adding one or two of these from the list can help tremendously. I read many of these suggested practices before sobriety, but I wasn't ready. This shift can only happen when you are ready. Even doing just one or two of these practices will add to living in joy, which is where I live today. I still choose to do many of them daily because they keep me on track and when I don't, I can often feel myself getting out of alignment with my highest self, with Source.

It is easy to fall off the path of emotional sobriety because there is negativity thrown at us constantly. There is a lot of noise, influence, temptation, and distraction in the world. Whether it's in our home, from a stranger on the street, a coworker, a community member, the news and television programs, the political climate, or anything else, there is so much to take in—too much. In case you feel like this too, I want to remind you that you get to decide how much of that you take into your heart.

It may be happening around you, but it is your inner work that dictates your inner world. You and only you control your inner peace. If you are taking on the options above in your daily life, the negativity of the world will sink you into an emotional pit. It doesn't even have to trigger you to pick up your proverbial bottle, or whatever the addiction might be.

It is important to me to help people gain their joy again. I speak most often about alcohol as it's what I know. I want to help people give up alcohol, but when they do, they often notice how they have transferred addiction elsewhere. Some other things we might find ourselves addicted to may include:

- Drugs
- Smoking
- Shopping
- Social media
- Religion/spirituality
- Video games
- Exercise
- Caffeine
- Sugar
- Eating
- Sex
- Work
- Drama

These are just to name a few. It is important to watch for our addictive behaviors showing up in other places and become intentional about healing and releasing the behavior of addiction, not just the substance we are addicted to. I used to live in negativity and play the victim. I was easily angered and did a lot of complaining. This was addictive because as long as I behaved that way, I didn't have to take responsibility for my life. I always found blame and just stayed "right" about how victimized I was. It took time and dedication, but I have overcome that negativity with these new practices in my life.

I had to go through a lot to shift from victim to survivor. When I started to move out of pity for myself, I had a real chance to heal and recover. It started slowly shifting my mindset and my relationship with life in general. It was amazing to find love for myself, and then for others.

This love of self and others is what carried the show, and my life, to its peaks. It's the same love that sustains me. As time went on, I relied on these practices to keep me aligned and empowered when the show's growth became overwhelming or challenging. For example, as I was evolving during the process, it came time to part ways with the producer. It wasn't the best fit and I relied on my faith and lessons in recovery to make the decision. Nonetheless, it was a difficult choice, and when I made the call to deliver the news, while I was on the phone, the lights started flickering in the room.

While I knew my decision was the right one, I felt affirmed when I saw the lights flicker. Had anything like that happened while I was disconnected from Spirit, I would not have noticed. In that decision, knew I would be alright and that whatever was next would show up along the path, and it did. Time and time again, the right things happened at the right time for the development of the show. Different team members, guests, viewers, and opportunities all popped up at the perfect time, or should I say in divine timing.

As the show continued to reach a larger audience, it went through an identity shift. I wanted to have a bigger impact, I was giving entrepreneurs and nonprofits a voice, but I wanted to move to a larger platform and empower more people. One year after the launch of *Coffee with Marci*, a rebrand was emerging. We got into a studio and joined a network called You Too America. With the new wave of interest and success, the show got a new name in August of 2019: *Wake Up with Marci*.

You might assume *Wake Up with Marci* would represent a morning show, but it means so much more. Waking up is in reference to becoming aware of your subconscious mind. It's a call to rise to our potential and start living with more intention. My show is an invitation to take a deeper look at ourselves and who we are in the world. Because of the work I had done, I have felt so empowered to spread as much awareness and light as possible. By the time of the rebrand, I was living a life beyond my wildest dreams, and I wanted to let anybody, and everybody, know that recovery, healing, and thriving are possible and available to all.

I was feeling more lit up and inspired than ever. The show still featured entrepreneurs, but I wanted to inspire and empower others through stories of hardship and triumph to spread hope. As a result of these transitions, the show spread more than just hope.

Wake Up with Marci spread across the tristate area by 2019, being broadcast on WLNY TV-CBS. It started to win awards and was featured in articles, exposing the show to a bigger audience, and also attracting and featuring more well-known guests. I was also being featured and winning awards, and the life I was living amazed me every day. Things were going so well, and I wanted them to keep going.

I knew I had to keep up my daily practice.

32

Flow Over Force

For a small portion of my recovery, specifically in 2019, I had very subtly transferred my addictive behavior to looking for, finding, and seeing the signs from beyond. Yes, even spiritual practice can become an addiction. In my business and personal life, I had developed a bit of an obsession with symbols that affirmed I was on the right path. I knew God had a plan for me, but I was always trying to detect and affirm it. It nearly turned into a scavenger hunt, always on the lookout for clues. Instead of enjoying the journey and going with the flow, I became hyper-focused on seeing the signs. I *needed* the affirmation.

Although well-intended, an addiction of any sort puts you into an altered state of mind. I had elevated from surprised and delighted to desperately seeking evidence before I would take any next step forward. It happened slowly and subtly, as addiction does. "Just one drink" progresses to "I can handle my drinking" then "I need a drink after a long day" and finally to full-blown alcoholism.

My frantic search for the signs started to become constrictive. I wasn't going with the flow, rather, I was sort of back in an old pattern of forcing outcomes and having expectations. I was committed to my emotional sobriety as much as my sobriety from alcohol so when I recognized this new habit taking shape, I recommitted to grace and surrender and let go of expectations. It wasn't easy.

I had to release my need to know back to God and realign myself with my trust in him. I had to surrender to life's unpredictability and trust that I was always on the path, whether I identified it or not. It's like when we plant a bulb. We don't see the plant come up immediately. We also don't dig to see if it has burst through its casing yet. We trust that given the right nurturing, it will come up and eventually bloom. Then we expect it to do it again the following cycle. We can revel in the joy it brings through the faith that we had for it to do what it was put here to do. Very much like our own lives. It was time to go back to being surprised and delighted, which I was able to get back to quickly once I recognized the pattern emerging.

That is something I would like to make special note of at this juncture: recovery isn't always flipping your life upside down. For starters, you don't always *have* to hit rock bottom, face first, to recover the quality of your life, and you don't have to stray too far when you get out of alignment. For example, when I stopped going with the flow and started forcing myself to see the signs, I was able to see the behavior before I spun out into making things up or seeing something out of nothing. I could have become so specific about needing signs that my life could have turned overwhelming or unmanageable again, but I didn't get to that point.

In fact, from the outside looking in, there was nothing wrong with seeking these signs. It was more of me noticing, "Hey, I am becoming a bit reliant on these symbols." It was simple enough to notice and simple enough to journal, get in communication, forgive, release, and realign. Said in much shorter terms: the more you do the work, the easier it becomes. Recovery smooths out along the way and gets easier as you go.

You are always surrounded by the harmony of the Universe. You are steeped in miracles, and it is when you open your eyes, ears, and heart to the magic of it all that it becomes obvious. Particularly when becoming sober, starting a new venture, or saying "yes" to something brave, you will be sent little thumbs-ups from God along your path.

Signs don't have to be grand; they could be in the form of a song that comes on at the right time or a word or phrase on the street with a message that means something special to you. When you feel like the message is speaking straight to you, it is, and it doesn't have to mean anything to anyone else. Universe brings into your experience exactly what you need to feel that affirmation or encouragement.

When I wanted to quit drinking I was bombarded with commercials, ads, and so much more. The message was always in my experience. God also speaks through others. This happens through a recovery program, social media posts, advertisements, a friend, family member, your spiritual director, or even a stranger. God will use all of his tools to reach and guide you.

One of the strangest ways that Source tried to reach me was in the winter of 2019. Ray was traveling, so I was home alone with the kids that weekend and they were already asleep. Late one evening, I woke up to let our dog, Lucky, out. Practically sleep-walking, I made my way back into the house. When we walked back in, our other dog, Cody, needed to go out, so I leashed him up and headed back out.

By then, I was just a bit more awake, but ready to get back to bed. When I came back in with Cody, I was startled by what I saw. In the hallway, where I had just walked through to take both dogs out, my work bag was sitting on the floor in the middle of the hallway.

Not only was my work bag inexplicably relocated, but my jacket that was previously hung up in the mudroom was placed on top of my work bag and it looked like a feather lying across the top of it. I was jolted fully awake by this and had the very clear thought that everything I was up to with my life and show were going exactly as they were supposed to.

I get goosebumps all over again as I write this because there is no explanation, other than God, that moved that bag and jacket to catch my attention. As I shared about my first live event, the feather was a clear sign to me that I am on the right path and that my angels are with me. When I saw that jacket in the middle of the hallway, I knew it was another validation from God to keep going.

If it weren't for my healing and faith, being home alone and something in the house being moved might have scared me. Because of my faith, I thanked God for the clear message, put my bag back up on the bench, prayed for a bit, and made my way back to bed peacefully.

The entirety of my talk-show journey has lined up perfectly with my sobriety journey. It is only the work of the Universe that could orchestrate all the wonderful ways it has turned out. I truly believe it is because I have surrendered my life to his will that the path is being laid out before me. The synchronicities of sobriety have been the blessing of a lifetime.

33

Finally Deciding to Write My Book

I must admit that I was a bit intimidated to write this book. I had been encouraged by others and even by Source. I felt the urge in me that I practically heard as a whisper from within: *Share your story.* Before I was ready, I questioned or second-guessed that nudge. I doubted if I could properly tell it or write it out. I wasn't sure it would truly portray my real-life experience.

One sunny Sunday afternoon, I had finally gotten enough nudges from my physical world and the nonphysical Universe. I felt myself surrendering to and affirming the guidance I had been feeling for so long. I walked out back and announced to the sky, "Okay God, I am going to write my book!" I felt a wave of relief come over me like I had set something free, like a caged bird had been released to fly, and no more than thirty seconds later, I was startled by the flapping of a dove's wings that had just landed on my roof.

I lost my breath at the physical confirmation of my energetic feeling. I think God wanted to be *perfectly* clear with me that day because he immediately followed up with a dragonfly zipping right past me which took my eyes off the dove and landed on a rainbow… get this… with no rain! A rainbow with no rain. That is the first and last time I have ever seen that, and I feel clear that God was confirming his will about me writing this book.

We are arriving at the end of these pages, but I want you to know that our time together doesn't have to end here. I would love to invite you to tune into Wake Up with Marci on WLNY-TV 10/55 in the tri-state area, CBS in Santa Barbara, Palm Springs, Idaho, and streaming on Hulu Live. No matter where you live you can watch the show, just check out www.WakeUpwithMarci.com for information and get more guidance from all of the amazing professionals, celebrities, and experts who share their stories of recovery, mental health, mindset, transformation, inspiration, education, and resources.

34

Mom's Passing

In my sobriety, I made a promise to Source—to God—and myself that I would surrender to his will for the rest of my life. Having a spiritual awakening because I worked through the steps in AA activated a commitment to carry a message of hope to alcoholics everywhere, and that morphed into spreading joy to anyone, regardless of whether or not they identify with being an alcoholic. During my time in the program, I often heard the reference *to serve*. There was no act too big or small that could change a person's life for the better, so being sure to take our time and attention to support one another meant everything.

As I remained consistent in my recovery, I transitioned my service from the AA meeting room to my home and then into my community. My life has become one of service in every capacity I can handle. I turned my life over to God and have learned to honor what I feel called to do. Every day is a chance to show up and do it again.

I had to use the steps of the program to look at how I lived my life and then work to fulfill what I now know was there all along, just waiting for me to wake up to it. I had many challenges along the way, but one of the biggest ones was the lesson of trust.

One time I had to put that trust to the test was in June of 2020 when my husband delivered the news to me that my mother, Rebecca, had passed away.

I had made breakfast and was sitting down to eat. My daughter was helping in the kitchen and my husband was on the phone outside. Right then, I was thinking how lucky I was—a delightful breakfast, my daughter helping me with unloading the dishwasher, and the beautiful view of the beach. I was feeling at peace.

My husband walked in and looked at me with a somber look on his face. My intuition kicked into high gear, and I knew something had happened. I looked at him with concern as my throat and chest got tight. His look made me nervous.

"I have something to tell you," he said in a sad, disappoint-ed tone. I stood up to face him, he grabbed my hands and held them tight. He looked me right in the eyes and said, "Your mom passed away."

I simultaneously yelped out a cry and fell into his chest. He embraced me with compassion as a huge wave of grief washed over me. It took over my whole body and I cried hard for about a minute.

With thoughts racing through my head, I tried to process what I had just been told. Naturally, I cried out of sadness, but more deeply, I knew I felt her peace. We stood there, Ray patiently and graciously holding space for my feelings, we experienced it, together. Being five years sober at this point, Ray and I learned to be better for and to each other. Learning to communicate healed so much between us and has carried us through some hard times. I am now able to trust, bond, and be vulnerable because I know how to truly share of myself.

As I started to relax, I thought to myself, *My mom is in Heaven. She is no longer struggling. She's at peace.* And I, too, felt at peace.

"It's okay," I said as I leaned away from my husband, looking him in the eyes. "She is no longer in pain. I no longer have to worry. She's with God now and she no longer has to struggle because of her addiction."

This kind of reaction to such news was relatively different for me in comparison to the earlier part of my life. When my father passed away, I spiraled out of control. I drank and did drugs to numb the pain. I regretted what I would never have. I was ashamed of my shortcomings. I longed for answers. I lashed out in anger at everyone and everything. Because of my healing and my beliefs, I was able to process the news differently, with a different understanding. I knew she was still with me, just not in her human form. She was on the other side, in peace, finally.

Because of my focus on healing in the last five years, I was also able to come to a place of acceptance and forgiveness in our relationship and my upbringing. I recognized that she never got clarity. She lived her entire life in chaos and used the only coping mechanisms she ever learned. My reactions and coping skills were healthier than they had ever been. I felt good about this and am eternally grateful for the healing and growth I have found.

That evening we went to dinner and sat around the table, reminiscing about my mom. During that time, my daughter Grace noticed a ladybug that was sitting right in front of her. Ladybugs are commonly known as the presence of a loved one who has passed on. I knew that was a sign from the other side that she was with us. It was the sign I needed at that exact moment. This brought an even deeper sense of peace and joy.

35

Mom's Presence

It was just a month after my mom's passing, and I was thinking about her frequently. Grief hit me in waves and without notice; I was having a harder time with her passing than I anticipated. My birthday was approaching, and it would be my first one without her. It felt empty and just "off" with her gone.

We went to our beach house for my birthday that year. I had a dinner planned with friends on one of my last evenings there after my workday. I had an interview earlier that day, so I put up a folding table to set up my camera and computer. I left my workstation set up and after the interview, got ready and headed out for dinner.

It was helpful to be surrounded by friends at that time. They knew I was having a hard time with my mother's passing, so they were sure to make me feel extra special. We had some laughs at dinner, and I felt celebrated and cared for. It was a beautiful night.

My family had gone back to our home ahead of me so when I returned to our beach house, it was empty. I walked into the upstairs living area and started to put away some gifts I had received. As I was picking some things off the couch, I noticed that a beautiful and inspirational piece of art, a Spiritile by Houston Llew, was missing. It sat on the table next to the couch, and it wasn't there. My heart dropped. I thought it had fallen and figured it was broken. I looked on the floor and it wasn't there. I was bewildered.

"Where could it be?" I asked myself out loud as I searched all around. It made no sense. *Did one of the kids move it? Did Ray?*

I sort of gave up finding it on the ground and when I turned around, it was lying on the table where I had set up my workstation. I did not have it there earlier during my interview. I walked over and picked it up. I could not understand how this happened. I know the piece of art well, but in that moment, it took on a whole new meaning.

It was a beautiful tile with a child on the front walking on the beach, with the saying, "When you need a miracle, just look at your child."

I lost my breath. I knew at that moment it was my mom. It was yet another message from the other side, a beautiful message from my mom.

I fell back on the couch with the tile in my hands, held to my heart, and said out loud, "I understand, you are with me. I love you," and I just cried. It is a memory that will stay with me for the rest of my life. True confirmation that she is with me.

I felt like my mom wanted me to know that she knew I was thinking of her, that she needed me to acknowledge that she was still present in my life. I also felt like the message of the frame expressed her joy for being my mom. We didn't have a perfect relationship, but she would always be my mom and I would always be her daughter. I surely felt close to her at that moment, and I often do.

The signs from the other side just kept coming. When I got back from the beach house, as I was telling Ray about the sign from my mom, a falcon sat and watched over us. We noticed it and watched it for a while. It felt more like it was watching us. It didn't leave for a long time. I felt its strong presence and I believe it was my grandpa's spirit joining us. I felt surrounded by family that week, which seemed to be just what I needed.

The promise I made to God is to trust. I promised to trust in timing and in outcomes to be exactly as they are supposed to be for my growth and greatest good. Yes, I had my feelings when my mom passed, but I was coping differently from in the past. When Ray and I faced tough times, I didn't default to a glass of wine or wishing to be out of the relationship; I didn't lash out in anger, repeating cycles of my past. When times and situations were challenging, I worked it out emotionally before addressing anything head-on. I checked in with myself and Source before reacting. I was seeing the signs and breaking the cycles in a once-and-for-all kind of way. I was transforming patterns that had previously run my life into the ground, and because of that shift, my life transformed for the better.

36

Living a Life Beyond My Wildest Dreams

Because of my commitment to and trust in my spirituality, I am living the best life imaginable. In fact, it is literally better than I could have ever imagined, and I can see it getting better each day walking this path. I want readers, listeners, and viewers of my content to know that I am saved by grace and that it is available for each of us.

I want to plant the seed that early trauma may have set in motion all kinds of addiction, and those cycles continue to repeat. I want to invite people to consider why their coping mechanisms are limited or why they automatically react a certain way instead of choosing responses.

There is a better way to live.

While not everyone needs a recovery program to break their cycles, they need something or someone to help them recognize what patterns they are repeating so they can address them. For example, we don't always see our reactions as negative, because we are blinded by our habits. Think of the person who experienced growing up with emotionally absent parents. Perhaps the parents were addicts (work or substance) and simply could not exemplify the full gamut of human emotions. The child learned to be stoic, to shut off feelings, to isolate, or distract themselves. Seems simple and safe, right? It was what they saw and how they learned. But in relationships, the person shuts down, leaves, or disappears completely into projects instead of talking through troubles. That person learned the mechanisms early on and cannot see beyond the confines of them. It takes another person to point out, either in a healthy way or by way of problems, how ill-equipped one is for handling challenges. Early intervention is always key.

In this example, imagine the person with the poor coping skills coupling with someone who was conditioned and raised like I was, where I raged and reached for a substance while looking for a way out. This person would never address the substance use, but instead would go deeper into isolation and distraction, creating more space until the person like me leaves. Two people with totally different unhealthy behavior cycles cannot just blend with each other. Whether people enter into recovery or therapy, cycles must be identified and reprogrammed.

Imagine another example: A person is recognizing they are living in stress at work. They cannot leave work at work, and depend on that job for a stable income, security, and health insurance. The stress is compounding with inflation, home repairs, unexpected medical challenges, or family problems. This stress has created anxiety where this person thinks of and dreads work. The person wakes in the night and thinks of the past, worries about the future, and cannot shut down the thoughts. The person wakes groggy and starts becoming more unproductive in a job that they don't enjoy. They need to cope. They need to sleep better, so they start having a cocktail in the afternoons. They get to sleep now, but it's a fitful sleep, and they wake up exhausted, so they turn to caffeine or other substances to jump-start the day. This interferes with the ability to focus. Perhaps this person goes to a doctor and gets a diagnosis and a prescription for ADD/ADHD, adult-onset, because they only explain the symptoms (inability to focus, hard time getting moving in the morning, hard time going to sleep, racing thoughts) instead of the cause (my job is terrible and I'm afraid to leave it). Now this person is dependent on not just the new prescription but also alcohol to wind down. The cycle repeats.

There is a better way.

Think of either scenario differently. What if either of them sought therapy? A therapist would recognize patterns and bring them into the open to discuss. The therapist may also ask for possible solutions which a person often knows but can't say out loud until asked in several different ways. Look at the person with the terrible job. A therapist could show the person that they are miserable in the job, and are using substances to cope with misery, but that those unhealthy coping mechanisms will turn into an addiction, and help the person find healthier ways to deal with the job (talk to management, create cultural changes within the company, create an exit strategy, etc.). Early intervention is key.

There is a better way to live.

I went from run-down, burnt out, living on repeat, and bottomed out to alive, healthy, wealthy, wise, and thriving. I started my own business, I continue to help others heal and grow, give back in any way possible, and more. I am the executive producer of a globally recognized show and now, I am a published author.

My marriage and motherhood are the healthiest they have ever been. I am the healthiest I have ever been. I talk to other parents and tell them what I've learned about my abuse and the signs that I sent out that people didn't recognize and didn't intervene. I advocate for our children and am doing my part to help end the abuse cycle. I help people around the world get the help they need to pull their life back together and find purpose in who they are. I live in deep gratitude for this life every single day. I believe this is one of the most powerful practices out there.

My hope for you, my dear reader, is that you found and felt the light and love of Spirit, however you address it, in these pages. I prayed over the message of this book that it would touch your heart in a healing way. I wrote with the intention of guiding you to a place within where you find your answers and individual connection with the Divine.

Thank you for opening your heart to this message. I want to remind you that help is always an ask away. You have people in your life who love you and you can always get the help you need. Thank you for investing your time in yourself to read this book. It is a clear sign of your self-love and desire to heal. I acknowledge you for that and encourage you to keep going. Stay faithful and God will continue to bless your path.

May God bless you, every day of your beautiful life. I wish nothing more for you than a life of peace, joy, and happiness. May you find your spiritual awakening; just ask and believe.

PART 6

Taking Action

Taking Action

There is so much more I'd like to share: about how to watch for signs of abuse in children and teens, self-help, what to do when you know someone is struggling with mental health challenges and crises, professionals that can help, support groups, and much, much more, so I've put together a sort of catch-all to end this book. These are nuggets that can be researched and expanded upon when and if they resonate or call to you in your journey.

I invite you to get a notebook, or even open a document on your computer as you read through these next few pages and interact with me. This will take some soul searching, and it may require some time to complete. Don't judge yourself. Whether you are on day one of your journey back to joy, or day one thousand, remember to be kind to yourself each step of the way.

For your convenience, I have italicized each of the journal questions or reflections.

Consider Your Past

The family dynamics of our formative years shape our survival strategies for life. I invite you to ponder how your upbringing shaped you, your outlook on life, and how you survived. Once you see the signs of your own negative survival tactics you can begin to make a change.

Reflect on your childhood.

When you think of your upbringing, what trauma or dysfunction did you endure?

Was it emotional, physical, control, neglect, sexual, instability, witnessing traumatic situations, or a lack of support, validation, or acceptance?

If your childhood involved and included toxicity on any level, you have learned survival tactics, and these are ingrained in your brain and nervous system. You have repeated patterns that you once used to deal with the chaos around you.

Here are six long-term effects of living in an abusive home:

- People raised in abusive homes will often engage in abusive relationships (either as abuser or victim).
- Children raised by a hypercritical adult are more often hypercritical of their children.
- Long-lasting trust issues. When raised by abusive adults, people learn to distrust parents, caregivers, and sometimes adults in general, as they learned that adults were not dependable or predictable, nurturing, kind, or—like in my case—unable to keep children safe and protected. This carries over into adulthood.
- Because a child did not have healthy role models, that person may grow up having difficulty expressing love or affection

and will often display poor boundaries.

- There may be a desire to detach from others, whether a partner, friend, or job. The mindset of hurting others before they can be hurt could become a coping mechanism.

- One may use numbing self, stuffing problems down, or masking them with substances or other addictions to avoid dealing with the pain.

When we are traumatized, we go into survival mode. And while this makes perfect sense during a threatening situation, these methods of survival can become ingrained and often hardwired.

The good news is there is help. Explore these thoughts and answer the following questions.

When is the earliest time you can remember a shift in your behavior?

What is the story you tell yourself about this incident or event?

What are the benefits and limitations of telling yourself this story?

This may have served you at one time; ask yourself: Does it serve a purpose now?

What actions or behaviors can you consider letting go of in order to live a more joyful life?

Are You Passing Down Positive or Negative Strategies?

If you are a parent, or an adult role model in any child's life, consider the ways you unconsciously pass down your generational pain onto the youth. It is more typical that we don't know we are doing this and pass down unhealthy beliefs or behaviors subtly and subconsciously.

Children do not know how to cope with adult pain or struggles. They don't need to. However, they do pick up on our anxiety, depression, and pain. They mimic us in many ways. They learn many of the same survival skills that we use and if we don't take responsibility for our negative coping skills, we can easily pass them down.

May you give the next generation the ability to thrive now. May you help yourselves, so you do not pass your pain and struggles down to your children. Today, there is greater awareness and acceptance of mental health issues. You can choose to heal. You can now seek help and break the cycle.

Here are some ways to help yourself break the negative survival practices.

- Practice forgiveness.
- Try inner child work. In this form of treatment, the unmet wants and needs of the child are brought back to consciousness and then resolved by gaining more knowledge of oneself, being aware of triggers, and establishing a sense of security
- Somatic therapy exercises may help you locate the stress in your body and work through the feelings.
- Mind and body practices such as exercise, eating well, getting plenty of sleep, and meditation.
- Find a therapist, watch videos from trusted experts, read self-help books, speak with a trusted confidant, or join a 12-Step

or other support program. Know you are never alone in your healing journey.

Take a few minutes and consider ways you may bring any of the above into your life.

Which might you implement immediately?

Which might you need more time to discover or research?

What might keep you from committing to any of the above?

Empowering Thoughts and Affirmations

We often are unaware of the looping thoughts that reside just underneath our consciousness. If we were told as children that we were loud, dumb, ugly, annoying, or any number of other negative adjectives, we may have begun to tell ourselves those same things.

Think of how you currently use self-talk.

If you miss a deadline, forget an appointment, drop a dish that results in a huge mess, or any other disappointing event, how do you speak to yourself?

In what ways does "wrong programming" show up in your inner thoughts and judgment of self?

If you are like many, you may have called yourself a derogative name or internally spoke down to yourself. It may reflect the way others responded to your accidents as a child. It may be the result of your putting high demands and expectations on yourself as a child.

Consider the root of negative self-talk: Where does it come from?

To counter some of the wrong programming, we must replace them with preferred, positive self-talk. Consider the following affirmations, and state them out loud.

- I am confident enough.
- I am kind enough.
- I am brave enough.
- I am smart enough.
- I am pretty enough.
- I am friendly enough.

- I am joyful enough.
- I am loving enough.
- I am nice enough.

Which of the affirmations felt "off" to state out loud?

Take a few minutes and journal about how it felt saying these, and which ones were harder to say.

Where did the feelings come from? Locate the source and explore.

These may not have resonated at all with you, and you may need to create your own or add to them changing them in some way. Feel free to use whatever language feels right for you. When writing your own, consider that you should feel something when you read your affirmations. When creating affirmations, use the above as a model:

- Keep them short.
- Say them as a fact not a possibility.
- Use present tense as if they are already true.
- Be persistent. Work with three to five positive affirmations at a time for a couple of weeks before switching them.

Write one negative self-talk statement you might say about yourself, then turn it around and state the opposite and in the present tense.

For example, you may have a hard time focusing on the good in your life and think that you have bad luck. Your inner critic may say, "My life sucks. Good things never happen to me."

Change your negative self-talk to positive affirmations by spinning it to: "I have a life of joy, fulfillment, and success."

Potential Signs of an Unhealthy Relationship with Alcohol

Whether you identify as an alcoholic or are experiencing alcohol use disorder or maybe you are considering changing your relationship with alcohol, here are some signs and suggestions for identifying and perhaps breaking the cycle.

> *As you read each of the following potential signs, respond in your journal by addressing where you believe yourself to be and how you feel about the following statements, i.e., whether they are true for you right now.*

- All your activities revolve around alcohol.
- You use alcohol to cope.
- You are impacting others around you by your drinking. For instance, always having to apologize for your behavior the night before.
- Poor sleep patterns. You may be able to fall asleep, but alcohol affects your REM sleep.
- Rapid weight gain or loss.
- Consistent hangovers.
- Increased or decreased tolerance.
- Shaky hands.
- Puffiness and/or chronic aches and pains.
- Stomach issues.

Suggestions for Helping Self

If you believe you have an unhealthy relationship with alcohol and you want to make changes, the following are prompts that may help you understand your alcohol use. Respond to journal prompts provided.

Identify triggers. Knowing what triggers a person to reach for a drink is on way to identify a trigger, and then seek healthier alternatives.

What are the precipitating factors for wanting a drink?

Practice curiosity. "Stop and think" instead of "react and drink."

Ask questions like "What is the lesson here?

Why am I angry?

What is really bothering me?

Do I really want a drink? Why?"

Watch out for old behaviors. We all have our ways of coping and many of them are self-destructive.

Make a list of these impulsive behaviors and have a plan for when you feel tempted to default to them.

What would be new, healthier behaviors that you could use when coping?

Change activities.

If you are cutting back or stopping altogether, what are some things you could do when faced with the desire and temptation to drink?

Keep a log of how many drinks you have in a given amount of time. This can also show the reality of consumption if approached with honesty. It's easy to lose track but when you count per day, per week, or per month, the numbers may tell a different story than you are telling yourself. Becoming aware brings light to areas otherwise hidden.

How many drinks do you think you have per week?

Begin tracking your alcohol use and write down how you felt before drinking, then after drinking.

In what ways did alcohol help or hinder the situation?

Consider cutting back or detoxing. Alcohol use disorder does not have to end with complete sobriety. There are new ways of approaching a healthier relationship with alcohol. If you want to cut back but not stop, start small. If you normally have two beers after work to wind down, consider just having one. If you drink three times a week, consider dropping to just two.

Sometimes, it is the people around who want to see the user change their ways.

In what ways would I like to change my use of alcohol?

In what ways do others desire for me to change my relationship with alcohol?

Why do I or others want to change?

If you decide to detox, please see a medical health professional. Ending substance abuse can have medical effects and it is important to make a change in a healthy, lasting way. There are substances that when abruptly stopped can cause death. Heavy drinkers who stop are at risk for experiencing delirium tremens which can be mild, like shakiness, to severe, like a complete cardiac collapse. This is not to be entered into lightly. Medical support is needed.

Get professional help. There are many free and paid resources but the help of a professional who is trained to help an addict get sober has the skill and resources to make a lasting difference. Therapy of all kinds is a two-way street. Commitment to change comes from within, then finding the right therapist, counselor, or life coach is essential.

How do I feel about therapy?

What would seeing a therapist mean for me?

In what ways would my life change if I sought help from a skilled professional?

Looking Back

To break any cycle, we must first identify, address, then meet that need for ourselves as adults. If we need to be heard, we must find someone who can listen. If we were neglected, we must find care. If we were abused, we must find the support to process and heal.

We must care for ourselves the way the little versions of us needed to be cared for.

If you are reading this book as part of your healing, consider what signs you may have put out for others.

What signals would have warned someone that you were headed down a dangerous road?

Meditation

One of the most valuable approaches to health and wellness is meditation.

How do you feel about meditation?

Have you ever had a practice before?

Who meditates?

How does one learn to meditate?

What does it mean to meditate?

I know a lot of people who do not make or take time for meditation because they think they don't know how or get bored by it. I know some don't because they are intimidated or avoid that kind of silence. I want to encourage you to include meditation in your healing journey because it is one of the most powerful tools we have.

Write down five beliefs you have about what it means to meditate.

Meditation will connect you to your Higher Power in a way that can remind you what you are made of. It can remind you of where you come from. It can show you what is possible, in and beyond this physical realm. I promise it is worth giving it a try and figuring it out.

There are a lot of guided meditations online, courses, books, and more. Many (but not all) yoga classes incorporate meditation but be sure you have done your research. You can also simply set a timer and sit still until the timer goes off. Sometimes you may even forget you have a timer in the first place! The goal is to let your thoughts just come and go without judgment and tune into your body.

I found an excellent meditation app to help me through trauma. Aura is an app designed to manage emotions and improve sleep through meditations, coaching, stories, and more.

What resources resonate with you?

Which do you believe would bring you more success: an online workshop?

A yoga class?

Self-directed meditation?

Complete silence or guided meditation?

Importance of a Routine

Research has yielded the importance of starting small but establishing routines if you are wanting to change your behaviors and the way you experience life.

How do you feel about routine?

What routines do you already have in place?

Do you wake up and reach for your phone? Does that serve you?

Do you drink coffee while scrolling through social media?

What do you currently do, and what would you like to do differently?

I offer you a daily routine that will put your healing journey into action. Do these at any time of the day that works for you. It is important to put our life into action to make a change. Routine gives you purpose.

All of these actions will help you to shift from thinking negatively about your life and raise your vibrational mindset to a more positive one.

1. When you wake up, don't dread the day. Welcome it by greeting your Higher Power with gratitude.

    What do you call your Higher Power?

    Write down what you could do differently upon waking to incorporate both the greeting and the gratitude.

2. Meditate for five to twenty minutes. Meditation teaches your brain to focus on the present instead of the past or future.

This can be through a guided practice or by sitting quietly with no distractions.

While there are countless guided meditations out there, here are a few of my favorites on YouTube:

Addiction: Spoken Meditation for Addiction read by Jason Stephenson, written by Amelia Schmelzer (March 21, 2016).

A Connection to a Higher Power: Connecting with God – Guided Meditation, Meditation with Holly (February 7, 2017).

Self-Care: 20 Minute Self-love Meditation: You are Worth It, Power of the Mind Meditation Club (April 13, 2020)

Release Negative or Trauma Energy: Clearing Negative / Trauma Energy from the Body, Guided Mediation, Suzanne Robichaud RCH (February 14, 2021).

Gratitude: Daily Gratitude Meditation-20 Minutes Meditation for Gratitude and Positivity to Start Your Day, Relax.Affirm.Manifest (August 17, 2020).

Choose one of the above recommended meditations and write down why you selected it.

Find a place where you will be undisturbed. Make yourself as comfortable as you can. Remember that meditation can be done in a number of positions. Prepare yourself, then complete the guided meditation.

Take a few minutes to come out of it, reflect upon it, then write what it was like for you.

Did you enjoy it?

What did you like and not like about it?

How can you see yourself benefitting from completing meditations like this?

Apps that I also recommend: Calm, Headspace, Healthy Minds Program

3. Consider the practice of keeping a gratitude journal or purchasing a gratitude jar and write at least five things you're grateful for each day.

What are you grateful for right now?

Did you wake up this morning?

Did you have a place to sleep?

These practices can be as simple as that. Consider all the things for which you are grateful in this moment. Write down a few.

Example: keep it simple.

- Thank you for my bed.
- Thank you for the roof over my head.
- Thank you for my clothes.
- Thank you for my eyesight
- Thank you for all of my limbs
- Or at the end of the day write things that you were grateful for.

4. Practice Breathwork. We take for granted our breath until it is compromised in some way. It is the very first thing we do when we enter this world and the last that we do before we die. The millions of breaths in between often go unnoticed. We have been told to breathe in through our noses and out through our mouths, but why?

What do you think about breath?

At what times do you find yourself thinking about, noticing, and paying attention to your breath?

Take a minute and answer those questions related to breath before reading on.

Breathwork can help you reach a deeper state of mind. Focusing on breath brings a person into the present moment. It is absolutely impossible to breathe into the past or the future. The breath is the anchor to the present moment. We often find ourselves caught up in anxieties (worry over what may or may not happen in the future) or depressive thoughts (mistakes we've made in the past, regrets, habits). The present moment and the breath that we have right now are all we are promised.

What does it mean to practice breathwork?

If you have never done it, what do you imagine it means?

In what ways can you imagine a benefit from practicing breath?

Write down how you feel about following a video on breathing.

Cue up the following video on YouTube: Five Minute Mindful Breathing, Epworth HealthCare *(October 3, 2019).*

After you have completed the practice, write about your experience.

In addition, how can you see yourself incorporating this type of work into your daily healing, or what might be a barrier to doing so?

There are many types of breathing exercises (sometimes called *pranayama*) that can be found in books and on the internet. Start small and be gentle with yourself. Remember to consult a medical professional if you have any specific health issues as certain types of breathing could be less effective than others.

5. Read Something Positive Daily. Just like starting any routine, it's important to start small and give yourself plenty of grace and time to get proficient. There are an infinite number of positive resources out there, so be sure to pick something that makes you feel good.

What flavor of positive do you prefer?

Are you religious?

Do you prefer science-based resources or even philosophical ones?

Take a minute to think about the style of writing that might attract you.

There are daily meditations, prayers, and thoughts.

There are weekly guides that might help.

There are even emails that are delivered right to your inbox!

What seems like a good fit for you?

Here are a few of my favorites: From Alcoholics Anonymous, *Daily Reflections* and *Twelve Steps and Twelve Traditions*. *The Daily Stoic* by Ryan Holiday and Steven Hanselman. *The Meditations* by Marcus Aurelius, adapted for the contemporary reader. *Lotsaholic* by Adam Jablin.

Do any of these appeal to you?

Where might you begin to search for something that does?

6. Feed Your Body Well. Think about your eating habits.

How do you describe them?

Do you eat three times a day at certain times?

Do you snack?

What does your daily intake include?

Consider keeping a log of this for a certain amount of time so you can be very clear about what you are putting into your body.

We need to fuel our bodies and brains. Be conscious about what you are feeding your body. Eating poorly leads to low energy, brain fog, and over time, may lead to potential disease. If you are in recovery, your body may crave alcohol if you are hungry, thirsty, or sleep-deprived. It's a great idea to keep up with what you eat, when, and how you feel afterward.

7. Exercise. A walk a day could be enough.

What is your relationship with exercise?

How often do you exercise?

What stories do you tell yourself about your level of activity?

Sometimes, just getting outside and walking for twenty minutes a day is enough to help shift the mindset and help highlight things to be grateful for. If you are interested in apps, here are a few I like: Nike Training Club, Strava, Aapptiv, Workout for Women: Fit at Home, and Peloton.

There are also many free exercise videos for all levels on YouTube.

What activities could you see yourself adding to your daily routine that are accessible?

What barriers can you imagine you may approach?

8. Get into Nature: Do a Technology Detox.

How often are you outdoors and present, free from electronic devices?

What outdoor activities did you once enjoy that you might be able to go back to?

How much time do you spend on devices (both for work and pleasure)?

Are you satisfied with that amount? In what ways does the use of technology add to your vitality or take away from it?

Consider disconnecting from your devices for at least thirty minutes several times a week and consider my favorites.

Which of the following seem like something you might want to try?

Can you think of other outdoor activities that would interest you more?

- Gardening
- Hiking
- Walking with your shoes off and feeling your feet on the grass
- Walking on the beach
- Lying in a hammock or reclining chair outdoors
- Meditating outdoors

9. Get Out of Your Head. Write the things you need to do that day on paper; get them out of your head so you do not worry about them.

How do you feel about setting goals and to-do lists?

Do they make you feel accomplished, or do they make you feel like a failure because you rarely finish the list?

Take a minute and write down one or two very small, tangible goals that can be attained before going to bed. For example, you might start with writing the following: eat a healthy meal; schedule the dentist appointment. Simple, short, sweet, and attainable.

This is setting small goals. If you do not get to one, don't berate yourself. Simply put it on the list for the next day. Celebrate the small wins daily. They are enough. This is called enjoying the journey.

Write down your commitment to setting small to-do lists or goals.

Start small. Perhaps you say: I commit to writing down my goals and to-do lists each morning for the next seven days. If I don't feel like they help me, I permit myself to drop the practice after seven days. If I skip a day, I promise to start again until I have done this consistently for seven days.

10. Acts of Kindness. Doing acts of kindness can boost feelings of confidence, being in control, happiness, and optimism. Our acts of kindness can be contagious! Do you hear of people who pay it forward in the coffee drive-thru lane? An act of kindness can inspire the recipient to then do an act of kindness for someone else.

When was the last time you did something for someone else without expecting anything in return (including a thank you)?

When was the last time someone did something for you?

How did it feel to receive a kind gesture?

Make your own list of acts of kindness you could give freely to others.

Some easy ideas

- give a compliment to a loved one or a stranger
- leave a note for a loved one or a friend
- call someone
- leave a big tip
- hold a door open
- let someone cut in front of you in a traffic jam
- lend a hand to someone at work
- look someone in the eyes and smile

Learning the Law of Attraction and Spirituality

One part of my healing journey has been spirituality and learning about the non-physical through Esther Hicks. The practices have allowed me to learn the law of attraction, manifestation, and moving into joy. I have learned that once I ask for something I want, and as long as I feel the emotion that it has already happened, I believe and trust the Universe that all necessary parts are being set up for me and my success. After I move into that vibration of truth, my life changed. Our life is full of goals. We may think certain things will bring us happiness. It is not money for the car in the garage that will bring us happiness, it is the belief in ourselves. Self-love and living in joy will make a difference. While I understand that not everyone believes in the law of attraction and manifestation, this is something that has worked extremely well for me, and I invite you to listen and see if it is something that works for you. In addition to multiple YouTube videos, there are books to help you learn the law of attraction and another way to live.

Esther Hicks is an inspirational speaker and author. She shares the teaching of Abraham through channeling and mediumship.

Abraham is "a group consciousness from the non-physical dimension." You can call it the Universe, Higher Power, Source Energy, Infinite Intelligence, God, or whatever you prefer, it doesn't matter.

In the books, the husband-and-wife team teaches practical spirituality. Their works are different from most other Law of Attraction teachers because they provide very hands-on techniques for using the Law of Attraction.

Although Esther Hicks and Jerry Hicks have written many, here are my favorite three: *The Law of Attraction: The Basics of the Teachings of Abraham; The Astonishing Power of Emotions: Let Your Feelings be Your Guide; Ask and It is Given: Learning to Manifest Your Desires.*

A Final Note

Please remember, I am just about seven years sober and have done a lot of work through my healing journey. Whether you are one day, one hundred days, or one thousand days into your journey, please remember to be extremely kind to yourself, forgiving, and take one day at a time. This is a lifelong venture and each step that you take towards a better, happier life is a win, and it should be celebrated daily.

To continue this journey with me, learn more about all I have discussed above, and see pictures please go to www.wakeupwithmarci.com follow the Chaos to Clarity page and get so many more resources. I can't wait to continue this journey with you.

About the Author

MARCI HOPKINS is an award-winning TV Personality; host and creator of *Wake Up with Marci* and a Recovery Expert on Fox, CBS, NBC and ABC.

Wake Up with Marci is a talk show - which airs on CBS owned WLNY-TV 10/55 in the Tri-State area and Streams on Hulu Live at 10 am on Saturdays. The show is also available on all Podcast Platforms. *Wake Up* is a talk show all about inspiration and empowerment. Marci shares stories of triumph and transformation to spread hope. She shares celebrity inspiration, spreads hope through triumphant stories, has Industry Leaders on to educate the audience and provide resources so the viewer can put their lives into action.

Wake Up is about living our happiest lives!

Marci has candid conversations with her guests and her mission is simple: She's committed to changing lives as an authority on recovery, spreading hope and happiness. She gives others' stories a voice. "My guests are living proof that it *is* possible to heal and that difficult situations do not have to define you...I hope viewers find strength, hope, and their purpose through these stories." The show is a passion project for Marci, who is six years sober after winning her battle with alcoholism.

When Marci's not hosting her show, the mother-of-two devotes much of her time to giving back to her community. Marci supports the Kumali Organization and other orphanages in Uganda, Africa. Since her fundraising efforts, one of the ministries has been able to buy land and build a home for the children. She is also on the board of the YWCA, dedicated to eliminating racism, empowering women, and promoting peace, justice, freedom, and dignity for all. The YWCA also helps women and children through Healing Space, helping those sexually assaulted. This is most important to her because she is a survivor of sexual abuse. Marci has also helped to open a safe haven for women and children in New Jersey through her interview and support of Access Family Services. Marci was awarded for her support. Marci has been honored as 2021 TOP 25 LEADING WOMEN ENTREPRENEURS by Leading Women Entrepreneurs, she has received the Women's Achievement Award from The New Jersey State Federation Women's Club, and was also honored by the Ramapo-Bergen Animal Refuge at their Whiskers and Tails Dinner and Casino Night.

Marci has been named a top influencer in New Jersey by 201 Magazine, featured on ABC, NBC, Fox, CBS, Yahoo, *CBS New York*; *PEOPLE en Espanol*, *Latina Magazine*; *News 12 NJ*; 201 Magazine, New Jersey Family Magazine, Hollywood Times, The Bergen Record, *BOLD Global* and other leading outlets. A native of Texas,

Marci started her career at Fox Cable Group, where she served in multiple roles and quickly climbed the corporate ladder, ultimately becoming the Director of On-Air Promotions for FX Network in Los Angeles.

Contact Marci Hopkins at wakeupwithmarci@gmail.com

For more great books visit
Books.GracePointPublishing.com

If you enjoyed reading *Chaos to Clarity* and purchased it through an
online retailer, please return to the site and write a review to help
others find this book.

Made in the USA
Middletown, DE
12 November 2023